GW00724836

A Little Touch of Harry

A Play

John Scholes

Samuel French – London
New York – Sydney – Toronto – Hollywood

ISBN 0 573 11246 0

A LITTLE TOUCH OF HARRY

First presented by Illawarra Spectrum Theatre, N.S.W. Australia on 19th August, 1983 with the following cast of characters:

Harry Ryder	John Scholes
Pauline	Margaret Burke
Allan Beaumont	Allan Ayre
Peter Ryder	Tony Newbury
Martha Ryder	Mary Petrie
Cheryl Bradshaw	Dorothy McDonald

The play directed by Marie Walsh

The action of the play takes place in Harry Ryder's flat in London and in an ante-room of a hired hall in Burnley.

ACT I	SCENE 1	Morning. Harry's flat.
	SCENE 2	A week later. An ante-room of a hired hall in Burnley
	SCENE 3	Early the following morning. Harry's flat. During this scene the lights are lowered to denote the passing of two hours
ACT II	SCENE 1	Later the same morning. Harry's flat
	SCENE 2	A week later—morning. Harry's flat

Time—the present

ACT I*

SCENE 1

A furnished flat in London. Late morning

It is a dingy little flat in a run down, neglected part of the city. There is a kitchen area up C where there is a window. A door L leads to a hallway and a door R leads to the bedroom. The room contains a large settee, a drinks cabinet, a table and chairs and a small table downstage R with a typewriter on it. There is a coffee table below the settee and an easy chair to the R of the settee

When the CURTAIN rises the room appears unoccupied. It is in a chaotic state due to a party the previous night. The chair normally by the typewriter is on its side in the middle of the room. The settee is overturned forming a pyramid and Allan Beaumont is asleep below it, completely hidden from view

Harry Ryder enters from the bedroom. He is in his fifties, wears a dressing-gown and slippers and appears to have a slight hangover. He surveys the mess, sniffs the stale air and opens the window

Immediately his ears are assailed by the wailing of a saxophone wobbling up and down the scales. Harry winces in exaggerated pain and firmly closes the window and eliminates the noise. He shakes his head to clear away the cobwebs and glances around the room. His attention is seized by the typewriter. He crosses to it and reads from the paper in the roller

Harry (*reading*) "Come in, Mr Steele, I've been expecting you." (*He repeats the phrase to himself a couple of times then looks around for the chair. He sees it, places it in front of the typewriter, seats himself and reads again*) "Come in, Mr Steele, I've been expecting you." (*He stops, hands poised over the keys. After a pause, he slumps back on the chair with a sigh of resignation and calls*) Cup of coffee?
Pauline (*off*) Please.

Harry goes to the gas stove in the kitchen area. He shakes the kettle, is satisfied there is water in it and places it on the gas ring. He searches around

---

*N.B. Paragraph 3 on page ii of this Acting Edition regarding photocopying and video-recording should be carefully read.

for some matches, muttering bad-temperedly. He bends over to look under the table

Harry (*shouting irritably*) Pauline! Where the hell are the . . . ?

A box of matches flies through the air from the bedroom and strikes Harry on his behind

(*Picking up the matches*) Thanks. (*He lights the gas under the kettle and throws the box of matches back into the bedroom. He shuffles back to the typewriter. He again sits down, with less determination than before, stares at the paper and reads aloud*) "Come in, Mr Steele, I've been expecting you."

Pauline enters from the bedroom. She is attractive, in her twenties or thirties and very self-composed. She stands in the bedroom doorway as she brushes her hair

Pauline Did you say something?

Harry (*with his eyes on the paper*) No, it was Prendergast.

Pauline (*looking over his shoulder*) It's over a week ago that Prendergast said that. What happens next? (*Brightly*) I know—why don't you have the goodies and the baddies making up and all going on a lovely trip to Toyland?

Harry Haven't you got anything better to do?

Pauline goes to the kitchen area and busies herself making coffee

Pauline Or you could have Prendergast fall in love with a delectable Salvation Army girl and . . .

Harry Lay off.

Pauline (*looking around the room*) Is there anything more depressing than the dead remains of a party?

Harry I had a good time. Didn't you?

Pauline Some of your friends, Harry! The only time we see them is when there's a booze up. Come and have your coffee.

Pauline places two mugs of coffee on the coffee table and perches on the overturned settee

Harry (*joining her*) What's the matter? Didn't Allan Beaumont pay you enough attention?

Pauline As usual, Allan Beaumont paid me far too much attention.

Harry And you're trying to say you didn't like it?

Pauline Allan gives me a condition something akin to creeping paralysis.

Harry You seemed animated enough in his company last night. You were dancing like a dervish with three legs.

Pauline I was in a dancing mood last night.

Harry So where's the paralysis? In your brain?

Pauline That's precisely where it is.

Harry Let's hope it doesn't move around to more important parts of your anatomy.

Pauline And let's hope you lose it from your typing hand.

Harry (*hurt*) Thanks.

Pauline I'm sorry, darling. (*She kisses him lightly*) Larry Steele will get us all out of the doldrums.

Harry And into what? Paradise?

Pauline Solvency.

Harry (*looking skywards*) And as the two enraptured lovers walked blissfully hand in hand out of the dark shadows of the doldrums into the warm, friendly rays of solvency which beamed down on them with ever increasing intensity ...

Pauline (*smiling*) It can happen.

Harry A pox on Larry Steele, Investigator Extraordinary.

Pauline He's done all right by you.

Harry One book! One sodding book! That's all the Larry Steele books that have sold and well you know it. That hardly makes me a second Conan Doyle.

Pauline You're the first Gerald B. Sharkey.

Harry Anyway, Larry Steele bores me to tears. I find myself more and more in sympathy with Boris Prendergast, arch evil genius.

Pauline You probably identify with him.

Harry Trouble is, after I've got him to blow up the world he'll have to find other planets to destroy.

Pauline Why don't you seriously consider the Salvation Army girl angle ... ?

Harry You're sending me up again.

Pauline Whatever happened to all that brash confidence you used to ooze with?

Harry It oozed itself into a mass of manure on my brain.

Pauline That should make it reasonably fertile.

Harry Only for weeds and creepy-crawly things.

Pauline Speaking of creepy-crawly things ...

Harry You're going to bring up Allan Beaumont again.

Pauline *You* brought him up last time.

Harry That wasn't Allan—it was prawn chow mein and five pints of lager.

Pauline I'm amazed. Do I actually hear you speaking in disrespectful terms of his holiness? He who can do no wrong?

Harry I'm only joking. Allan's all right.

Pauline In his place. But he can't ...

Harry Stay locked in a sewer all day ... I know, I know. ... You've said it many times before and no doubt we'll hear it again.

Pauline I finished with Allan three years ago.

Harry To come and live with a broken-down old coot like me.

Pauline Harry, you've got to stop all this self-denigration. It's not like you.

Harry (*rising, jovial*) Right. No more self-inspecting, circumspecting introspection. It's back to bad, bold, blazing Harry Ryder of yesteryear that everyone knows and loves.

Pauline That's it—confidence.

Harry (*looking skywards*) With confidence and ecstasy lighting up their faces the two lovers walked through the forest of despair and gloom to bravely encounter the perils and tribulations that confronted but never daunted them.

Pauline (*rising then kissing him*) Now, how about getting some clothes on and popping down to the corner shop for a few things. Hard though times are, we must eat.

Harry (*moving towards the bedroom*) Right.

Pauline (*calling him back*) Oh, Harry, give me a hand with the settee, will you?

Together they pull the settee to its rightful position. They do not notice Allan Beaumont, fast asleep, cuddled up to a cushion with an empty glass in his hand

Harry exits through the bedroom door

Pauline tidies the flat. She finds Harry's shoes under the typewriter table

Harry (*off*) Pauline! Where the hell are my ... ?

Pauline throws his shoes into the bedroom and moves to the kitchen sink

Thanks!

Harry's shouting rouses Allan Beaumont. He sits up on the floor and blinks at his surroundings. Pauline has her back to him at the kitchen sink. Pauline turns to continue her tidying up, sees Beaumont and screams

Harry dashes in from the bedroom wearing a shirt and with his trousers round his ankles. He pulls up abruptly as he sees Beaumont

(*To Pauline*) I told you not to rub that old lamp too hard.

Pauline I just turned over a rock and there he was.

Beaumont I'm glad you did. I might have hibernated for the winter. (*He gives his glass to Pauline*) No more for me, thanks.

Harry (*pulling up his trousers*) We've just been talking about you, Allan. Did you ... er ... hear any of it?

Beaumont Not a word.

Harry is relieved

I've been waltzing away in the arms of Morpheus ever since that fat bird put a hammerlock on me.

Pauline (*picking up a handbag lying beside Beaumont*) No wonder she was giving you the works. It looks as though you've pinched her handbag.

Beaumont Not guilty. I wouldn't even pinch her bottom and she's got acres to spare.

Harry (*helping Beaumont on to the settee*) Pauline, brew something for the lad. Can't you see he's suffering?

Pauline (*coldly*) I would have thought he'd have wanted to get to his own home as soon as possible—it's only a block away.

Beaumont (*rising*) Perhaps I will ...

Harry (*pushing him down*) You stay there. (*In a hard voice*) Pauline ...

Pauline puts the handbag on the drinks cabinet and goes to the kitchen area

Pauline Yes, O Mighty One?

Beaumont (*rising*) I think I'd better ...

Harry (*pushing him down*) You stay there. You know you're always welcome here. Isn't he, Pauline?

Pauline grimaces

Beaumont You're very kind, Harry. But I'm sure you can do without a hungover business manager just now.

Harry You're a friend, Allan.

Beaumont And you're the best friend a fellow ever had, Harry. I think the world of you ...

Pauline Sugar?

Beaumont What?

Pauline Do you want sugar in your coffee?

Beaumont Er ... yes. Two please. Have you forgotten? (*To Harry*) As I was saying, from the first there's always been a special place in my heart ...

Pauline Black?

Beaumont Pardon?

Pauline Do you still like your coffee black?

Beaumont Er ... yes. (*To Harry*) As I was saying, I'm very fond of you both. You're a real man's man and Pauline ... well, she's such a ...

Pauline Tart?

Beaumont What?

Pauline Would you like a jam tart?

Beaumont No thanks. (*To Harry*) How's Larry Steele's latest epic adventure coming along?

Harry (*lightly*) Oh, it's bursting through on the rails.

Beaumont When do you think it will reach the finish.

Harry Oh, soon.

Pauline It's being jostled on the turn at the moment.

Beaumont (*smiling*) But the winning post's in view, eh, Harry?

Harry It's an odds-on certainty for a fast finish.

Beaumont Let's just hope there isn't a protest.

Harry tiredly rubs his forehead

What's the matter?

Harry It's just that I've run out of racing terms.

Pauline (*handing Beaumont a cup of coffee*) How about—Harry Ryder wins by three falls to one?

Beaumont That's wrestling—isn't it?

Pauline Harry, don't forget you were going to get some things from the shop. (*She eyes Beaumont*) On second thoughts *I'd* better go.

Harry (*cheerfully*) You stay here and keep Allan company. (*To Beaumont*) You'd rather talk to Pauline than me, wouldn't you, you licentious sod?

Beaumont 'Course I would. You push off, you clapped out old bugger.

Harry and Beaumont laugh lightly at the exchange

Pauline (*impatiently*) When you two old cronies have finished your mutual back slapping ...

Harry (*crossing to the bedroom*) I'll get my jacket.
Pauline There's a list of things we need on the bedside cabinet.

Harry exits through the bedroom

Beaumont Lovely cup of coffee.
Pauline (*moving about as she tidies up*) And it's free—like the booze you guzzled last night.
Beaumont (*wincing*) Don't mention last night.
Pauline All right—I won't.

Harry enters. He wears a jacket and holds a carrier bag

Harry Right—I'm off. (*He goes to the door* L) I'll be careful crossing roads and I won't talk to strangers.
Pauline (*kissing Harry gently*) There's a good little boy. I might have something nice for you when you get back.
Harry (*with a wide grin*) I'll work up an appetite.

Harry exits L

Pauline crosses to the kitchen area and looks busy

Beaumont (*after eyeing her steadily for a few moments*) You can drop the act now.
Pauline What act?
Beaumont This "Allan Beaumont is a slimy toad" act.
Pauline I thought that was *your* act.
Beaumont On the contrary, I thought I was always nice and decent with you—and with old Harry, of course.
Pauline (*going to the* R *of the settee*) Look, Allan, whatever your act is, please drop it.
Beaumont (*with a deep sigh*) We were friends for a long time, Pauline. How long was our blissful relationship?
Pauline Eighteen months.
Beaumont I've never stopped being very fond of you.
Pauline Oh for God's sake, Allan, how long do you intend to trot out the same, meaningless rubbish?
Beaumont Until you come back to me.
Pauline Then you'll prattle away forever. I'm devoted to Harry.
Beaumont (*sneering*) Devoted . . .
Pauline Harry thinks the sun shines out of you.
Beaumont 'Course he does. Aren't I the one who got his one and only pathetic little spy novel published? And aren't I the one who introduced him to the most gorgeous woman in his life? And isn't he the ungrateful bastard who took that said gorgeous woman away from me?
Pauline When will you come to terms with the fact that it was *I* who willingly came to live with *him*?
Beaumont But—why?
Pauline I've told you a hundred times.

Beaumont I've never managed to get you alone a hundred times since we broke the spell.

Pauline I want what's best for Harry—let's leave it at that.

Beaumont (*crossing to the typewriter*) All right, but you don't convince me. (*He reads*) "Come in, Mr Steele, I've been expecting you". (*With derision*) Stirring stuff. He hasn't a cat in hell's chance of having another book published—and you know it better than most. I think he knows it, too. (*He sits on the settee*) Meanwhile, I suppose you'll continue to support him like the naïve little angel you pretend to be. Where are you working now? In a bookshop, isn't it?

Pauline keeps her back to Beaumont

Oh well, whatever makes you happy makes you happy—as my dear departed grandmother used to say. She was full of wise sayings like that, my grandmother. Another of hers was, "When darkness falls, look for a lighthouse." She was dead right, of course. You'd have liked my grandmother. She used to keep grandfather's ashes in his favourite tobacco jar. I suppose I'm a bit like my grandmother—I like to cling to ashes, too. Would you say that's a fair assessment?

Pauline ignores Beaumont

Another of hers was "Don't judge a bird by the droppings he leaves." She certainly had a grip on life, my grandmother. She kept a grip on grandfather, too. (*He turns to Pauline*) I've finished my coffee.

Pauline moves below the settee to take the cup from the coffee table but Beaumont grabs her outstretched arm and pulls her on to the settee. She struggles but he manages to kiss her. She slaps his face but he keeps a firm hold of her

Pauline Let go.

Beaumont (*flushed from the battle*) Oh Pauline, have a little sense. I love you.

Pauline (*more loudly*) Let go.

Beaumont Be reasonable. I only want to ...

Harry enters L carrying the groceries which he places on the table near the door

Harry Everyone rejoice. I'm back.

Beaumont (*to Pauline, pretending*) So then she grabbed hold of me like this—and put a grip on me something like this—and I was helpless. Oh hello, Harry. That was the quickest shopping spree I've ever known. (*He releases Pauline*)

Harry Hardly a spree. Only three items.

Pauline (*quickly going to the shopping bag*) You didn't get the butter.

Harry It's not on the list.

Pauline Yes it is.

Harry hands her the list

Oh well, I obviously forgot. We must have some.

Harry All right . . .

Pauline (*quickly*) No. I'll go.

Harry But . . .

Pauline (*emphatically*) I'll go. There are other things we need. (*She collects her purse from the bookshelf then kisses Harry*) I won't be long.

Pauline exits L

Beaumont rises and crosses R

Harry puts his jacket on the back of the chair and moves below the settee

Harry What was all that about?

Beaumont What was all what about?

Harry (*pointing to the settee*) The gymnastics.

Beaumont Oh that? I was telling Pauline about that giantess who confronted me last night. What was her name?

Harry Sylvia.

Beaumont That's it—Sylvia. (*He laughs*) Frightened hell out of me.

Harry (*laughing*) What did she do?

Beaumont How do you mean?

Harry You were telling Pauline what she did. So . . . tell *me*.

Beaumont (*dubiously*) Er . . . um . . . she sort of held my neck and . . . sort of . . . my arms . . . and . . .

Harry That's not how you were telling it to Pauline.

Beaumont Er . . . no. I was sort of . . . demonstrating.

Harry Well . . . sort of demonstrate on me.

Beaumont (*offhand but nervous*) You don't really want me to . . . do you?

Harry (*coldly*) I insist on it.

Beaumont (*going to Harry*) Well . . . she sort of . . . (*He pushes Harry's arm up his back*) . . . then she sort of . . . (*he puts his other arm around Harry's neck*) Like this.

Harry (*composed*) Then what?

Beaumont Nothing else. Well, that is—I don't want to hurt you.

Harry Did you hurt Pauline?

Beaumont No.

Harry Perhaps you were just coming to the rough stuff?

Beaumont (*touching where his face was slapped*) No, we'd already been through it. I mean . . .

Harry So what did she do?

Beaumont Who?

Harry Sylvia.

Beaumont Oh. Well, she . . . sort of . . .

Harry breaks Beaumont's grip and puts the same grip on him—but much firmer

Harry (*in a very matter of fact voice*) Now let's get this right. She held you like this?

Beaumont (*nearly choking*) Y . . . yes.

Harry Then did she do this? (*He rams Beaumont's arm further up his back*)
Beaumont (*in pain*) Y . . . y . . . yes.
Harry Then this? (*He kicks Beaumont's feet from under him*)
Beaumont (*on his knees. Worried*) S . . . s . . . something like that.
Harry Then I suppose she did something like this.

Harry lifts Beaumont to his feet and then throws him with a flourish. Beaumont does a somersault and lands painfully on the floor

Beaumont (*grimacing with pain*) I don't think you quite captured the delicate nuances of it all but that's as near as damn it.
Harry (*advancing on him*) Did she try this one . . . ?
Beaumont (*rising swiftly*) I think that was the lot. Rest assured, Harry, you've made your point.
Harry (*satisfied*) Well, Sylvia will probably be calling around to get her bag. I suggest you vacate the premises—unless you want a repeat performance from her.
Beaumont That—I can happily forego. Give her a half-nelson from me. (*He moves to the door* L)
Harry Be seeing you, Allan.
Beaumont Lovely party, Harry. You're a great guy. (*He opens the door*) Oh, and good luck with the writing. I know it will be a sensation. What's it called again?
Harry *Save a Bullet for Me.*
Beaumont (*savouring it*) *Save a Bullet for Me* by Gerald B. Sharkey. Great. It's got "Book of the Month" written all over it. Well, thanks again. Bon Savlon.
Harry Abergavenny.

Beaumont exits L

Harry crosses to the typewriter

(*Reading*) "Come in, Mr Steele, I've been expecting you." (*He sits at the typewriter and seems about to type. He shakes his head and rises. He crosses to below the settee* L *and muses aloud*) "Steele's alert eyes caught the glint of light on a knife held by his would be assailant, Kronos, behind the door." (*He shakes his head*) No. He'd be a bloody fool to try that again. Not after he got his testicles mangled by the same tactic in chapter two. (*Thinking aloud*) Prendergast's beautiful agent, Zarina de Vote, stood at his side with a wicked-looking Luger in her hands." (*He goes purposefully to the typewriter and sits down. He shakes his head*) No. The only thing she'll hold again is a harp. Steele threw her from the top of the Eiffel Tower in the last chapter.

There is a knock at the door

Sylvia, come to collect. (*He takes the handbag from the drinks cabinet and crosses to the door* L. *He holds up the handbag and grins as he opens the door*)

Peter Ryder stands in the doorway. He is in his early twenties, soberly dressed and is acutely embarrassed and gauche

Harry registers shock as he stares at Peter

(*Dumbfounded*) Peter?
Peter Hallo, Dad.

After a pause Harry lowers the handbag

Harry I suppose you'd better come in.

Peter enters. He wanders C R of the settee. Harry throws the handbag on the table upstage L. Peter half smiles as Harry eyes him, grim-faced with suspicion

Do you intend this to be a fleeting visit or do I ask you to sit down?
Peter Thanks Dad. (*He sits on a chair*) Nice place.
Harry (L *of the settee*) It's a bloody awful place.
Peter (*trying to joke*) Yes, on second glance it's not exactly the Burnley Kierby hotel.
Harry (*with annoyance*) I could have bet my last pair of woollen socks you'd mention Burnley within sixty seconds of entering this place. What am I supposed to say now? How is everyone? How's dear Uncle Simon and Aunt Lil? How's little cousin Tommy? Have they straightened cousin Vikki's teeth yet? How are the great bunch of blokes at Fowler's Engineering Limited? How's the weather up there?
Peter You could say, "How's Mum?"
Harry And I could have bet my last pair of wellies you'd mention her within minutes.
Peter What do you expect?
Harry I certainly didn't expect to find you on my doorstep.
Peter You don't think we can avoid talking about Mum altogether, do you?
Harry I most certainly do. And if you intend to discuss her you can clear out of here right now.
Peter Haven't you even the slightest interest?
Harry I've stayed away from her for five years. Does that suggest interest to you?
Peter (*rising*) Come on Dad. It's hard enough for me to face you like this without you getting bitter.
Harry (*as if explaining to an infant*) Peter, you are part of my past now. A very large part but one I want to forget. You're a very nice fellow and I have nothing against you but you must realize that I have drawn a very definite dividing line between the life that was and the life that is. You, unfortunately, are on the other side of that line and if I am to have peace of mind you must stay there.
Peter Dad, don't you think you've taken all this a bit too far? After all . . .
Harry It's no good, Peter. It wasn't just her. Twenty odd years as a works accountant. The sheer, agonizing boredom of it.
Peter But that's got nothing to do with Mum.
Harry I only slogged away at that lousy company to give her all the little niceties her heart desired. And in return she gave me nothing.

Peter That's not true, Dad. She loved you very much. And still does.

Harry Her kind of love is one of slow suffocation. Selfish and demanding.

Peter But after over twenty years of marriage couldn't you discuss it like civilized people?

Harry Ahh. I *did* the civilized thing. I left her. When I tried my hand at writing a novel and it was accepted I knew where destiny lay.

Peter But you're still married.

Harry True. But you are forgetting that dividing line. (*He sits on the settee*)

Peter Well, I think it's a damn shame.

Harry Naturally. I bet she's given you a grim account of her sufferings over the years.

Peter I told you—she loves you. She cries a lot even now.

Harry (*sneering*) She was always expert at turning on the waterworks.

Peter (*going towards Harry. Nervously*) Dad ... I don't how to say this ...

Harry (*suddenly*) Drink?

Peter Er ... no ... I don't ...

Harry (*crossing to the drinks cabinet* L) I don't know if there's any left but I could do with one at this moment. (*He takes a bottle of gin and two glasses from the cabinet*) Go on. Have a drop of something.

Peter (*sitting on the settee*) Well, if you've got any sherry or something ...

Harry (*doubtfully*) Sherry? Well ... (*He spies a bottle sticking out of the soil in a large plant pot upstage* R. *He crosses and takes out the bottle. He brushes off the soil and examines the label*) Vermouth! (*To Peter*) Vermouth?

Peter Well ... all right.

Harry crosses to the cabinet and pours the drinks

Dad ... I'd better tell you why I'm here ...

Harry hands Peter his drink and sits next to him on the settee

Harry By the way, my whereabouts are supposed to be a secret. How did you know where I lived?

Peter Mum gave me your address.

Harry Well how did she ...

There is a knock at the door

Harry puts his drink on the cabinet and opens the door L

Pauline enters with the groceries which she puts on the table near the door

Pauline Forgot my key. (*She smiles and nods to Peter. To Harry*) Well, that didn't take too long, did it? It's not a bad sort of day. Bit breezy. Allan Beaumont's blessed us with his absence I see. Really Harry, when are you going to have a shave and make yourself look nearly human? (*To Peter*) Excuse me, I won't be a minute.

Pauline exits into the bedroom

Peter's wide eyes follow her and then he frowns at Harry

Harry merely smiles back at him. He takes his drink and sits on a chair obviously enjoying Peter's confusion

Pauline returns, nods and smiles at Peter again and starts putting the groceries in a cupboard in the kitchen area

Pauline (*looking at Peter*) Have I met this friend of yours before, Harry?
Peter No ... I'm ...
Harry (*with mock formality*) Pauline, this is Peter Ryder. Peter, this is Pauline.
Pauline Peter Ryder? (*With a squeal of recognition*) You're Harry's boy. How lovely to meet you. (*She advances towards Peter*)

As Pauline advances towards him Peter extends his hand for a formal greeting but Pauline puts her arms around him and hugs him tightly. Peter manages to turn his head towards Harry and raise an eyebrow but Harry is used to Pauline's effusive greetings and he continues to smile at Peter. Pauline stands back and surveys Peter

Well, what a wonderful surprise. I've heard a lot about you.
Peter Really? (*He shoots a glance at Harry*)

Harry avoids it, loses his smile and feigns disinterest

Pauline Come and sit down.

Pauline leads Peter to the settee and sits next to him on his R

If you encounter any stray bodies flaked out under the furniture don't think it's because I'm a careless housekeeper. So ... you're Harry's boy. Well ... well.

Peter gives an embarrassed smile

How are things in ... where do you live?
Peter Burnley.
Pauline Oh yes.
Peter Things are fine.
Pauline What do you do?
Peter I'm an accountant.
Pauline Really? Not for Harry's old company, by any chance?
Peter As a matter of fact, yes.
Pauline Do you hate it as much as Harry did?
Peter No—I can't say I do. But then, that would be difficult.
Pauline (*laughing*) True words. What's that you're drinking?
Peter I think it's called vermin or something.
Pauline (*laughing*) Vermouth. Well I don't normally drink at this time of the day but I'll make an exception in this case.

Pauline crosses to the drinks cabinet closely watched by Peter who, in turn, is closely studied by Harry. Peter casts a glance at Harry who turns away with an air of indifference. Pauline returns to the settee with a drink
(*Sitting*) Cheers.

Peter Cheers.

Harry mutely raises his glass in a toast and drinks

Peter (*to Pauline*) Do you live with . . . er . . . live here?
Pauline Yes. I hope you're not shocked.
Peter (*quickly*) Oh no. (*On reflection*) I suppose I am a bit surprised. But no
    more surprised than Harry . . . I mean Dad, when I put in an appearance.
Pauline (*laughing*) I can imagine. You and your mother are supposed to be
    part of his buried past, you know.
Peter Yes, I know.
Pauline How is your mother?

*Harry gives out a loud, emphatic cough. They turn to him. He gives a silly little
smile and an equally silly wave*

Harry Remember me? Dear old dad?
Pauline (*returning his silly wave*) Hallo, dear old dad. (*To Peter*) I think
    he's feeling neglected.
Harry I was wondering when all this nauseating gush was going to subside.
Pauline When Peter and I have got to know each other.
Peter Well, I hate to throw cold water over such heartwarming matiness but
    I have work to do. (*He points to the typewriter*)
Pauline I'm sure it can wait, darling.

Harry goes to the drinks cabinet and pours a drink

Harry (*emphatically*) No—it can't.
Pauline The typewriter is in *that* direction, O great one.
Harry (*bad-tempered*) Well, I'm having a booster first. Do you mind?
Pauline (*to Peter*) You'll have to excuse your father, Peter. He's not getting
    anywhere with his writing and it's making him a bit peevish.
Harry (*warningly*) Pauline . . .
Pauline (*rising and facing Harry defiantly*) You haven't seen Peter for five
    years. You could show him a little warmth.
Harry (*shouting*) And I made it quite clear to Peter that I wouldn't care if I
    don't see him for another five years. Or ever again.
Pauline (*shouting*) Even you can't be that callous.
Harry Just you watch me.
Pauline The charm just pours out of you, doesn't it?
Harry This calls for honesty—not charm.
Pauline Then why don't you *be* honest?
Harry (*angrily*) All right, I will. (*To Peter*) Peter—push off.

Peter rises

Pauline (*pushing him back*) Stay there Peter.
Harry Oh I see. You want me to be tactful? (*To Peter. With mock sweetness*)
    Peter, my boy, it's been absolutely lovely seeing you again and it was nice
    of you to call but I'm afraid that pressures of work make it necessary for
    me to ask you to leave. I'm sure you understand.

Peter rises

Pauline (*pushing him back*) Stay there, Peter.

Harry I'm not in the habit of repeating myself, Peter.

Peter (*rising*) I think I'd better go.

Pauline (*pushing him back*) Stay there. (*To Harry*) I think you should be ashamed of yourself.

Peter (*rising*) I really think I ought to ...

Pauline (*pushing him back*) Stay there.

Harry This is my flat and he is ... (*His voice trails off*)

Pauline Your son. Harry, he isn't the landlord after the rent we owe or a debt collector wanting his pound of flesh. He's your son.

Harry All right, all right. You've made your point.

Peter (*rising*) I think I'd better go.

Pauline (*pushing him back*) Harry's going to be nice. Aren't you, Harry?

Harry (*sighing*) Yes. I'll be nice.

Pauline (*to Peter*) Would you like another drink?

Peter (*with admiration in his eyes*) Yes, thank you.

Pauline takes his glass and her own to the drinks cabinet

Pauline (*pouring the drinks*) Harry, darling, the air's very stale in here. Could you open the window?

Harry opens the window. The air is rent with the sound of a saxophone going over the scales. Harry closes the window quickly

Peter What was that?

Pauline Young Alistair in the flat opposite. He's been practising those scales for an eternity.

Peter It must drive you mad.

Harry It does. But someday he'll master the instrument and we'll hear nothing but sweet music.

Peter If he sticks at it.

Harry Exactly.

Pauline gives Peter a drink and sits beside him on the settee. Harry wanders down R

Pauline You haven't told me why Peter is here.

Harry He hasn't told me yet.

Pauline (*to Peter*) Is there a reason?

Peter (*uneasily*) Well ... there *was* a reason ... but ... let's forget it.

Pauline Was it something important?

Peter (*awkwardly*) It seemed important ...

Pauline Come on, Peter, tell us. We're all agog.

Harry For heaven's sake, Pauline—if he doesn't want to tell us he doesn't want to tell us. I'm not as agog as all that.

Pauline But he's come a couple of hundred miles for something. (*To Peter*) Well?

Peter Well ... all right.

Peter produces an invitation card from his pocket and places it carefully on the coffee table. He takes a big gulp of his drink. After a pause, Harry picks up the card and reads it. He stares hard at Peter who looks steadfastly into his glass

Harry (*in outrage*) No! (*He slams the card on the coffee table and stalks to the window and stares out*)

Pauline reads the card

Pauline (*handing the card to Peter*) Congratulations.
Peter Thank you.
Pauline Who is she?
Peter A girl I met at work. We've been going together for about six months now. (*To Harry*) Dad ...
Harry No!
Peter I was just going to say I understand. You don't have to come to the engagement party.
Harry That's just as well, because I'm not going.
Pauline (*firmly*) Of course you are.
Harry There is nothing you can say that would induce me to go—so don't try.
Pauline (*in a raised voice*) Now you listen to me, Harry Ryder ...
Peter It's all right, Pauline. I didn't really expect him to go. But Mum and I thought it would be nice to ... well ... extend the invitation, so to speak.
Harry The three of you make me sick. (*He moves L of the typewriter*)
Pauline (*crossing to Harry*) Why?
Harry Don't think I can't see through this diabolical little scheme.
Pauline What do you mean?
Harry (*moving to Peter*) Your mother found out my address somehow ... I don't know how, but she did. Why didn't she post the invitation? Why send you all this way?
Peter Well, Mum thought ...
Harry (*sneering*) Mum thought. I bet she thought. She thought the sight of you with a pathetic little invitation to an engagement party would melt my flinty old heart, didn't she?
Peter It's not like that at all.
Harry Isn't it? I think it is. (*Mimicking Peter*) "She cries a lot. She still loves you." God, Peter, you must think your old dad's a bloody fool.
Pauline What are you getting so frenzied about?
Harry I just want it established that I am not taken in by Martha's subterfuge, that's all.
Pauline But what have you got to be afraid of?
Harry Who said I was afraid?
Pauline No one. But you're acting like Peter had handed you your death warrant instead of a chance of eating cheeseballs and trifle.
Harry Why are *you* so keen to see me go?
Pauline For God's sake, it's only an engagement party.
Harry It's more than that.
Pauline Rubbish.

Harry You must see as well as I do that this is the thin end of the wedge.

Pauline You still haven't explained why you're afraid.

Harry I am *not* afraid.

Pauline You seem to be afraid to me. (*To Peter*) What about you, Peter? Does he seem afraid to you?

Peter Well, I must admit he does seem a bit . . .

Harry (*exploding*) You stay out of this.

Pauline (*admonishing*) Harry . . . losing your temper won't solve anything.

Harry There's nothing to solve. I'm resisting the overpowering temptation to gorge myself on cheeseballs and trifle. (*To Peter*) Tell Martha to stick them up her . . .

Pauline Why don't you tell her yourself?

Harry (*frustratedly*) Oh . . . go to hell.

Harry storms into the bedroom R *and slams the door*

Pauline (*shouting to Harry*) You don't seriously believe Peter's fallen in love with . . . (*to Peter*) What's her name?

Peter Er . . . it's Cheryl.

Pauline (*shouting to Harry*) Cheryl . . . just so that he could lure you back into Martha's clutches, do you?

Harry opens the door

Harry (*with his head through the doorway*) I wouldn't put it past him.

Harry returns to the bedroom and closes the door

Pauline (*shouting to Harry*) But you've always said Martha is better off without you.

Harry opens the door

Harry But the thought that I might be better off without her would make her choke on her cocktail franks.

Harry returns to the bedroom

Peter (*shouting to Harry*) But *are* you better off?

Harry re-enters

Harry You stay out of this.

Harry returns to the bedroom

Pauline (*shouting to Harry*) But why should she want you back?

Harry re-enters

Harry I'm not saying she'll succeed.

Harry returns to the bedroom

Pauline (*shouting to Harry*) Then what are you saying?

Harry re-enters

Harry That a prisoner who has managed to escape doesn't meekly give himself up to go back behind bars.

Peter He does if he's starving and cold.

Harry I can assure you, son, that my escape has not resulted in me being starved or cold. What is more, I quite enjoy being at large.

Harry returns to the bedroom

Pauline You're still Peter's father.

Harry re-enters

Harry So I'll send him a telegram.

Peter Dad ...

Harry Does the message, "A bird in the bush is worth two dozen in Barnoldswick" sound nauseating enough?

Peter Dad ...

Harry No. You're right. It does lack a certain piquancy.

Harry returns to the bedroom

Pauline I'm just saying that next Saturday you ought to be at your son's engagement party.

Harry re-enters

Harry (*angrily*) You can say what you bloody well like—I am not going.

Harry returns to the bedroom and slams the door

Pauline (*calling*) Harry ... you're being very childish about all this. (*There is no response*) You know that, don't you? (*There is no response*) Martha's been dead to you for five years. What harm can a dead person do you? (*There is no response*)

Pauline and Peter exchange glances

Peter I'd better go.

Pauline He thinks it's a plot.

Peter I know.

Pauline Finish your drink.

Peter No thanks. I've gone off it. I feel as though I've made a mess of things. I'm sorry ...

Pauline Don't apologize. (*She moves to Peter*) And don't worry. He'll show up next Saturday.

Peter I'll be very surprised if he does.

Pauline (*emphatically*) He'll be there.

Peter Anyway, I'm not sure now that I want him to show up.

Pauline (*quickly*) Don't be silly. He must be there.

Peter But I wouldn't feel too good if he came because he was forced into it.

Pauline Are you having second thoughts?

Peter I suppose I am.

Pauline What if I told you he really wanted to see Martha again?

Peter Judging from what I've just seen I'd say you were high on "vermin".

Pauline Possibly. But it's true.

Peter You've got to be joking.

Pauline We'll see.

Peter (*moving to the door* L) All right.

Pauline Peter . . .

Peter Yes?

Pauline (*crossing to him*) Is it true what you said to Harry?

Peter What?

Pauline Your mother still loves him? Cries a lot . . . that sort of thing?

Peter Yes . . . it's true.

Pauline How has she been surviving?

Peter I earn a decent living.

Pauline What about Cheryl?

Peter Oh, she's all right.

Pauline I mean . . . you'll soon be married. What about her then?

Peter (*pondering*) Well . . . I suppose . . . she'll have babies . . .

Pauline (*patiently*) Your mother.

Peter Oh . . . well, Uncle Simon's been very good to her since Dad . . . well, it seems Uncle Simon nearly married Mum instead of her sister, Aunt Lil.

Pauline Does she get a lot of support from him?

Peter Well, they've got a lovely big brick home in Brunshaw Road called "Simlil" and . . .

Pauline (*patiently*) Your mother.

Peter Oh . . . yes. A little bit.

Pauline Sure you don't want to finish your drink?

Peter (*tempted*) I . . . (*he looks towards the bedroom*) I think I'd better go. (*Plucking up courage*) I'll say one thing. I think Dad's very lucky. You're . . . very nice.

Pauline (*smiling*) You admire his choice?

Peter Yes . . . yes, I do.

Pauline Goodbye, Peter.

Peter (*holding out his hand*) Goodbye.

Pauline suddenly embraces Peter. She gently pushes him through the door and closes it

She smiles to herself as she resumes putting the groceries away

Black-out

SCENE 2

A week later

The Lights come up only on stage R. This area now represents an ante-room of a hired hall in Burnley. There is a small table which holds various engagement presents. There is the faint sound of a band playing

As the Lights come up Martha Ryder is standing beside the table, holding a coffee pot. She is in her forties and is well-dressed

Cheryl Bradshaw enters R. *She is in her early twenties and is attractive but slightly tarty*

Cheryl How are you feeling now, Mrs Ryder?

Martha (*holding up a coffee pot*) From Len and Pat. Nice, isn't it?

Cheryl Yes. I've seen it.

Martha You know Len and Pat Billings, don't you?

Cheryl No, I've never met them. Peter's mentioned them on occasions.

Martha Nice couple. Len works with Peter ...

Cheryl Yes ... Peter said.

Martha (*holding up the present*) That's very nice. It will be useful.

Cheryl Yes ... Mrs Ryder, how's your headache?

Martha No better, I'm afraid, Cheryl.

Cheryl Oh dear.

Martha They've got a lovely home at the top of Mosely Road.

Cheryl Who ... ? Oh ... er, Len and Pat Whatsit?

Martha Billings. Len's really doing well. Nice couple ...

Cheryl Look, Mrs Ryder, if you don't feel up to joining the party ...

Martha Not just now, Cheryl. I'd ... I'd rather just stay here for a little while.

Cheryl I think that might be wise.

Martha Is he ... is he ... er ...

Cheryl Still here?

Martha Yes.

Cheryl Yes ... he is.

Martha Oh dear ...

Cheryl (*patting Martha's arm*) Look, if you're not feeling well there's no earthly reason why you should have to put up with his drunken stupidity.

Martha Is he ... is he ... er ... ?

Cheryl He's getting worse if anything.

Martha Oh dear ... what's he doing?

Cheryl The last I saw him he was sitting over in a corner with his feet up on a table.

Martha Drinking?

Cheryl Naturally.

Martha Oh dear ...

Cheryl (*smouldering*) The nerve of the man.

Martha I suppose ... in a way ... it was to be expected.

Cheryl He was already three sheets to the wind when he got here. And he's been attacking the punch like a demon possessed.

Martha Lil made the punch. She's very clever at that sort of thing.

Cheryl It's not good enough ...

Martha Don't let Lil hear you say that. She's very proud of her punches.

Cheryl Your old man, I mean. It seems to me he only came here to cause trouble.

Martha Let's not talk about him (*She holds up another present*) From Ken and Rosemary. Nice, isn't it?

Cheryl Very nice.

Martha Rosemary's expecting her second.

Cheryl It makes me so mad . . .

Martha Do you know Ken and Rosemary Tattersall?

Cheryl Er . . . no . . . I don't think so.

Martha I think you do.

Cheryl Do I?

Martha Greengrocers on Park Road. Nice house up Brunshaw way.

Cheryl Oh, them.

Martha (*holding up the present*) You should be able to find a good use for this.

Cheryl Shouldn't it have an attachment?

Martha Should it?

Cheryl All the ones I've ever seen have an attachment.

Martha Really? Perhaps they come separate.

Cheryl You can get them at Hardacre's with it already on.

Martha Really?

Cheryl I'm not sure what it's supposed to do, though.

Martha Well . . . it . . . er . . . Lil's got one. Ask her.

Cheryl (*agitated*) I'm not going to speak to him if he's going to carry on like that.

Martha Hardacre's is a good store. You can generally find what you want there.

Cheryl It would have been better if he'd stayed in London where he belongs.

Martha Don't think about him, Cheryl. This is your big day—your engagement party. Look at the lovely presents you've got.

Cheryl (*unsure*) Well . . .

Martha What's Peter up to?

Cheryl Dancing attention on everybody.

Martha I suppose it's his big day too.

Cheryl Then you'd think he'd show a bit more interest in me.

Martha (*friendly*) Plenty of time for that later on.

Cheryl I suppose . . .

Martha Are your mum and dad enjoying themselves?

Cheryl As much as anyone can with him around.

Martha That's a lovely dress your mum's wearing. I could never wear pink.

Cheryl I just hope he doesn't hang around too much longer.

Martha Pink's an unlucky colour for me.

Cheryl I still think he shouldn't have been invited.

Martha Did I ever tell you about that pink chiffon ball gown I once had?

Cheryl Yes, yes you did.

Martha Brought me nothing but bad luck. Harry liked it, though. No . . . I tell a lie . . . it was the yellow one he liked. Anyway, I remember once wearing it to a dance at the Mechanics' Institute . . .

Peter enters. He wears a suit and tie and is agitated

Peter Mum—when are you coming out of here?

Cheryl She's got a headache.

Peter Still?

Cheryl Still. And anyway, why should she go out there?

Peter (*nonplussed*) Why should she? Because ... for heaven's sake, Dad's out there.

Cheryl That's right.

Martha (*to Peter*) Cheryl tells me he's behaving very badly.

Peter Not really ...

Cheryl Like hell he isn't.

Peter Nobody'll talk to him.

Cheryl That's because he's behaving badly.

Peter Why didn't you stay and talk to him after I introduced you?

Cheryl I wanted to talk to your mother.

Peter Mum ... please ...

Martha I'm not feeling well. Perhaps later. (*She holds up a present*) From your Aunt Lil and Uncle Simon.

Peter Very nice. Look, Uncle Simon's talking to Dad now ...

Cheryl I thought you said no one would talk to him.

Peter (*to Martha*) You know what Uncle Simon's like.

Martha I know what your father's like.

Peter Exactly.

Martha What do you expect me to do?

Peter (*sighing*) Just come out and say hallo to him.

Martha I've already said hallo to Simon.

Peter Don't be awkward, Mum. You know what I mean. Say hallo to Dad.

Cheryl And get her head bitten off?

Peter Look ... he's as docile as a lamb.

Cheryl Hah ... that's a laugh.

Peter Just give him a chance ...

Cheryl Have you gone deaf or something? Your mum said later.

Peter Do you want this party to be a success or not?

Cheryl Don't ask stupid questions, Peter.

Peter All I can say is it'll turn into a free-for-all riot if Dad's left alone with that lot out there.

Martha I'm not accountable for Harry's behaviour.

Peter We're accountable for the crockery.

Martha Don't exaggerate, Peter.

Cheryl And stop pestering your mum like this.

Peter shrugs hopelessly and exits

Martha (*picking up the present*) Are you sure Hardacre's have them with the attachment?

Cheryl Pretty sure.

Martha You'd have thought the Tattersalls would have got one with an attachment.

Cheryl Probably got it on special.

Martha Probably.

Cheryl I've heard they're a bit on the mean side when it comes to dipping into their pockets.

Martha Yes ... I've heard that too.

Cheryl All airs and graces.

Martha And they must be worth a lot.

Cheryl Mum says they've just had double glazing put in.

Martha That's not cheap.

Cheryl And you know where they're going for their holidays, don't you.

Martha No. Where?

Cheryl Switzerland no less.

Martha They went to Denmark the year before last.

Cheryl You'd think they could afford one with an attachment.

Peter enters, more agitated

Peter It's on. It's on. I knew it would be on. I said it would be on and now it's on.

Martha ⎫
            together What's on?
Cheryl ⎭

Peter Nobody ever listens to me.

Cheryl Peter ... calm down.

Peter He's just a stupid, ignorant oaf.

Cheryl I told you that from the start.

Peter Not Dad—Uncle Simon.

Martha They're not—fighting?

Peter Not yet.

Martha Harry's got such a violent temper.

Peter Then Uncle Simon shouldn't provoke him.

Cheryl Shouldn't you be out there keeping the peace instead of beating a retreat in here?

Peter I'm supposed to be at my engagement party—not refereeing a wrestling match.

Martha I just hope Simon restrains himself.

Peter Mum, please—come and see Dad.

Martha Well, I ...

Cheryl (*to Peter*) The man's drunk, throwing his weight around and behaving like a complete pig and you want your mum to risk life and limb ...

Peter Now who's exaggerating?

Martha I'll wait until he calms down.

Peter I've tried to talk him into coming in here to see you.

Cheryl Well, if he won't make a move, why should she?

Peter (*sighing*) I'll try again. (*He looks through the door*) Oh God—now Aunt Lil's having a go at him.

Peter exits

Cheryl (*angrily*) My engagement party—he's deliberately trying to ruin it.

Martha Don't let him get to you, love. (*She holds up the present*) You might be able to take this back to the shop and exchange it for one with an attachment.

Cheryl I don't know which shop they got it from.

Martha Baxter's, It's on the box.
Cheryl Oh? They're a bit out of the way.
Martha I'll take it back for you if you like.
Cheryl That's very good of you, Mrs Ryder.
Martha You'll have to start calling me Mum.
Cheryl Well ... Mum, I want to thank you for everything.
Martha Nonsense ... I'll see to it that you get an attachment.

Peter enters even more agitated. He has a glass of punch in his hand

Peter I give up. I give up.
Cheryl What's the problem now?
Peter This is beyond me. Completely beyond me.
Cheryl What's he up to now?
Peter I've no idea.
Martha What have you got there?
Peter (*forgetting himself*) What's it look like?
Martha (*affronted*) Peter!
Peter (*with chagrin*) Sorry Mum ... it's a glass of punch. I need it.
Martha You're not used to it.
Cheryl (*to Peter*) Like father, like son.
Peter You'll be relieved to know that Dad's taken the hint.
Martha He's left?
Peter Right—left.
Cheryl Good riddance.
Peter And Aunt Lil's having a fit of the vapours.
Martha (*quietly sobbing*) I feel this is all my fault.
Peter Don't think that, Mum ...
Cheryl (*to Martha*) You did the right thing. You invited him and he abused your hospitality.
Martha (*taking Peter's hand*) Peter ... I'm so happy for you.
Peter (*awkardly*) I ... I'm so glad ... Er ... how's your head?
Martha Better.
Cheryl (*to Peter*) I hope you've seen your father for what he is.
Peter Yes ... yes, I have. (*He drains his glass and turns*)
Martha Where're you going? Not to look for him?
Peter For a recharge. It could do with a touch more "vermin", though.

Peter exits

Cheryl Come on, Mrs Ryder ... er, Mum. You haven't met my brother Craig.
Martha Is he the one in the army uniform?
Cheryl That's him.
Martha He bought you the toaster.
Cheryl Let's take the presents out.

Martha and Cheryl each take an end of the table and carry it towards the door

Martha Geoff and Susan bought you a toaster as well.
Cheryl Geoff and Susan?

Martha The Hardcastles from Briercliffe. It's not as nice as the one Craig bought you, though.

Martha and Cheryl exit with the table

Black-out

SCENE 3

Harry Ryder's flat. Early the following morning. It is about 1 am

The room is empty and in darkness. The curtains are drawn and the bedroom door is ajar. There is a knock at the door L. *Short pause. The knock is repeated*

Pauline (*off*) I'm coming.

There is another knock on the door

(*Off*) All right, Harry, I said I'm coming.

Pauline enters from the bedroom. She wears a very flimsy nightdress. She rubs sleep from her eyes as she switches on the light

One of these days you'll remember that key of yours ... (*She opens the door*)

Peter enters hurriedly. He is still wearing his suit

PETER!

Peter (*rushing to the* R *of the settee*) I'm sorry to charge in on you at this time of night but I must see Dad. (*He turns to see Pauline's inadequately covered body. This adds to his already substantial agitation*)

Pauline (*with amusement*) No dad here. Will I do?

Peter (*gawping at her despite his attempts to look elsewhere*) No dad here?

Pauline I think I said that.

Peter But he must be here.

Pauline (*going closer to Peter. Mockingly*) Oh, well, if you say he *must* be here then let's find him. (*She searches in unlikely places, cupboards, drinks cabinet etc., calling*) Dad ... dear old dad. Come on out, dear old dad ... we know you're here somewhere. (*She manages to brush up against Peter several times as she roams the room*)

Peter watches her with interest

No dad in this room. (*She points to the bedroom*) Want to help me search in there?

Peter (*seeing he is the butt of a joke*) All right, all right. But have you any idea where he might be?

Pauline I should have thought you'd be in a better position to answer that. After all, it's your engagement party he's been to. Or has he?

Peter Oh, he came to the party all right. Worst luck.

Pauline sits on the settee drawing her knees under her chin. She smiles alluringly at Peter

Pauline I thought it was dear old dad at the door. That's why I didn't go to any trouble to cover up my charms.

Peter (*from behind the settee and looking down on Pauline's low-cut nightdress*) I can see them ... er ... that.

Pauline My sense of the dramatic tells me you must have quite a story to tell. (*She pats the settee beside her*) Come on, let's hear it.

Peter paces up and down

Peter (*confused*) You haven't seen him in the last few hours?

Pauline You take some convincing, don't you? I haven't set eyes on your father since I gave him a soldier's farewell at Euston Station this afternoon. (*She looks at her watch*) Yesterday afternoon.

Peter (*unsure*) I see. What should I do now?

Pauline That's up to you.

Peter I'd better go and come back some other time.

Pauline Don't be silly. You can wait here.

Peter But we don't know how long he'll be.

Pauline He won't be long.

Peter How can you be so sure?

Pauline (*smiling serenely*) I know my Harry.

Peter Well ... I don't know ...

Pauline (*suppressing her exasperation with difficulty*) How can I get you to relax?

Peter (*tensely*) I am relaxed.

Pauline (*patting the settee*) Then sit down.

Peter perches on the arm of an easy chair. Pauline smiles and continues to pat the settee beside her. Peter rises, smiles and takes a step towards her. Suddenly he breaks towards the door L

Peter I think I should go and look for him.

Pauline (*sighs*) Where? The Zoo? Westminster Cathedral? The Battersea lock-up?

Peter He might have had an accident.

Pauline Where did you get your medical degree?

Peter I'm sorry but ...

Pauline Stop apologizing. (*She rises, takes Peter's hand and leads him to the settee*) Don't you think I'm ... nice, any more?

Peter (*sitting on the settee*) 'Course I do ...

Pauline Then will you please pay me the compliment of refraining from treating me as though I was a cannibal with a knife and fork and a jar of pickles.

Peter I'm sorry ...

Pauline (*at screaming point*) And stop apologizing. Now ... what can we do to while away the time? Any ideas?

Peter's gaze is magnetically drawn to Pauline's cleavage

Peter Do you want to hear what happened at the party?

Pauline (*with mock surprise*) Whatever gave you that idea? (*Thinking hard*) I know ... I spy with my little eye something beginning with ... T.

Peter looks at Pauline's barely concealed breasts

Peter (*after a pause*) Pauline ...

Pauline No—that begins with a P.

Peter Speaking of which, I ...

Pauline (*pointing to the door* L) It's through there to the left.

Peter No ... not that. Speaking of names, I only know you as Pauline.

Pauline (*moving closer to him*) Oh ... you're trying to get on a last name basis with me?

Peter I was just wondering.

Pauline Trousers.

Peter (*frowning*) That's your last name?

Pauline No—that's something beginning with T. Your turn.

Peter Oh.

Pauline (*looking around thinking*) O ... ? uhm ... er ... ornament? No ... ? er ... ottoman. ... Settee? No ... er ...

Peter I didn't mean O, I just meant ... Oh.

Pauline ... Organ?

Peter I can't see an organ.

Pauline No, neither can I.

Peter Pauline ...

Pauline Operation scar ... ? No, you can't see that either. (*She looks down*) Or can you?

It is now Peter's turn to be exasperated. He is vaguely aware that Pauline is deliberately sending him up

Peter Pauline ... don't you want to hear the story?

Pauline 'Course I do. (*She rises*) But to help your faculties I'll put something a little less—shall we say—titillating—about my person. Make some coffee.

Pauline exits into the bedroom

Peter is a little troubled. He goes to the kitchen area, shakes the kettle, is satisfied it contains water and puts it on the gas ring. He looks round for the matches

Peter (*calling as he looks under the table*) Pauline! Can you tell me where I can find the ...

A box of matches flies in from the bedroom and strikes Peter's behind. He picks them up

Thanks.

He lights the gas. He idly looks around the room and ends up at the typewriter

(*Reading*) "Come in, Mr Steele, I've been expecting you." (*He repeats the phrase a number of times with different accents and emphasis*)

Pauline enters. She wears a housecoat over her nightie. She also wears slippers. She moves R of the easy chair

Peter moves to the L of the settee

Pauline Well, I must admit I'd sneakingly hoped I'd see you again.
Peter I hoped that, too.
Pauline And here we are.
Peter Yes . . . here we are.
Pauline (*moving to Peter*) Take your jacket off, make yourself comfortable. (*She helps him off with his jacket and places it on the back of the settee*) Have you been drinking, by any chance?
Peter (*defensively*) Well, I have been to a party.
Pauline I'm not condemning, only observing.
Peter You should have observed me a few hours ago—I was really in a bad way. The drive here has sobered me up.
Pauline And what earth-shattering experience turned an abstainer into a skid row candidate?

Peter puts his hand to his eyes and shakes his head in self-pity

Peter Oh, Pauline, it was unbelievable.

Pauline seats him on the settee and sits beside him. She loosens his tie

Well, the party was in a hired hall. It was in full swing when he got there and by the way, he was so definite last week he wouldn't go and yet he did. Did you have anything to do with that?
Pauline (*smiling*) Powers of persuasion.
Peter You must have plenty of it.
Pauline And I'm capable of using it to good effect.
Peter Well I was flabbergasted when I saw him walk in the main door.
Pauline (*rising*) Kettle's boiling. How'd you like your coffee?
Peter Milk, no sugar thanks.

Pauline makes the coffee in the kitchen area

Pauline Go on.
Peter What?
Pauline Your saga of life with father. Your flabber had just been gasted— go on from there.
Peter He was already three parts full when he got there. Said he couldn't go past the *Adelphi Hotel* without popping in for old time's sake. Then he downed gallons of punch and started insulting everyone in sight. Everybody was trying to be friendly and I was going bananas trying to keep the peace. Then he got to grips with Uncle Simon.
Pauline And there's no love lost there.
Peter It was no contest really. I must say Dad made a real fool of him. (*He smiles*) Uncle Simon was crimson in the end. He told Dad he was a shiftless queer. That's when he copped the contents of the punch bowl down the front of his trousers.
Pauline Accidently, of course. (*She sits next to him with the coffee mugs*)

Peter Right. Then aunt Lil had a go at him. Said he should have stayed away where he belonged. That's when she found strawberry mousse on her flowered hat.

Pauline Where was your mother while all this was happening?

Peter She spent the whole time Dad was there in an ante-room with Cheryl and the engagement presents. I kept trying to get her to meet Dad—then trying to get Dad to see her, but neither would budge that last few steps. It was a bloody nightmare.

Pauline So the twain wouldn't meet? I can understand Harry's behaviour—to a point—he'd fulfilled his contract by turning up. But why did your mother act like that?

Peter She said she had a headache and couldn't face him. Anyway, while I was in with Mum, Dad stormed out and just . . . disappeared. I felt so bad about the way things had turned out that I ended up drinking too much. Then I decided to drive here and apologize to Dad about everything.

Pauline I'm only guessing—but wasn't it your mother's plan to get him there in the first place?

Peter That's what I told her—I've given up trying to figure people out.

Pauline (*smiling alluringly*) Have you tried to figure me out?

Peter Funnily enough, you've been on my mind all week.

Pauline (*close to him*) And what conclusions have you reached?

Peter I don't know. You're a bit of a . . .

Pauline (*helping*) An enigma?

Peter Something like that.

Pauline Do you think I'm wicked?

Peter Why should I think that?

Pauline (*seductively*) Because I am.

Peter (*looking hard at her*) No you're not.

Pauline (*gritting her teeth*) Don't bloody argue with me, Peter, I said I am.

Peter All right. I believe you.

Pauline Don't you think it's wicked to steal a man from a respectable wife and family?

Peter Yes, but Dad didn't leave Mum for you. He came to London to take up writing. He hadn't even met you then.

Pauline But she wants him back.

Peter Yes.

Pauline And if he didn't have me he'd go back.

Peter I'm not so sure about that.

Pauline You haven't had a great deal of experience with women, have you?

Peter (*slightly taken aback*) Well . . . er, I've had some . . .

Pauline Come on. You've never been as close as this on a settee with a wicked woman before.

Peter (*unsettled*) 'Course I have.

Pauline Really? And what did you do?

Peter I can't see what . . . I mean . . .

Pauline Were all those women enigmas like me?

Peter Some were a bit funny.

Pauline So what did you do?

Peter (*uncomfortably*) I don't know ... I can't remember. Look, how long do you think Dad will be?

Pauline You are a sly one.

Peter (*puzzled*) Me? Why?

Pauline Admit that Harry's still in Burnley and you knew very well he wouldn't be here tonight.

Peter Why should I come here then?

Pauline You knew I'd be here. You said I'd been on your mind all week.

Peter Yes ... I know, but ...

Pauline (*becoming aggressive*) And you've been close to wicked women before.

Peter Yes ...

Pauline What did you do, Peter? (*Her face is tantalizingly close to Peter's*)

Peter Look ... I admit you were right. I haven't had a lot of experience with women. But ...

Pauline (*warming to her task*) What would you *like* to do, Peter?

Peter (*after an agonized pause*) I spy with my little eye something beginning with ... B.

Pauline (*unrelenting*) Bedroom door.

Peter suddenly stands and crosses R of Pauline

Peter (*agitated*) It's not true what you said, you know.

Pauline (*with a deep sigh*) What isn't?

Peter I didn't know Dad wouldn't be here. He's not in Burnley ...

Pauline I'll accept that. He's gone missing before. In circumstances like these he usually seeks solace from his male friends. They drink, play cards and discuss the treachery of women.

Peter I thought you'd be his usual source of solace.

Pauline You forget ... it was me who talked him into going to your party. He's probably sticking pins in a doll the image of me right now.

Peter More likely the image of me.

Pauline Anyway, you can be sure he'll be gone all night.

Peter (*dumbfounded*) You said he wouldn't be long.

Pauline (*innocently*) Did I? When?

Peter When I first came in.

Pauline Who knows what the fates have pre-ordained?

Peter I can't work you out.

Pauline That's what comes of being an enigma. It's very sad really.

Peter Well, I keep thinking about Dad.

Pauline (*changing tactics and becoming emotional and weepy*) Your father hasn't given you a second's thought in five years. You didn't exist for him.

Peter In a way, I can understand that.

Pauline And what about me? He blamed his failures in the last twenty odd years on a frigid and uncaring wife. Once he realizes the truth—that he's a failure in this new life—where does that leave me?

Peter Why do you stay with him?

Pauline (*with a slight sob*) I suppose I needed to feel I was an inspiration to someone creative.

Peter What about now?

Pauline (*sobbing miserably*) Needs change.

Peter (*concerned, he sits next to her on the settee*) I thought you were happy together.

Pauline (*wrapping her arms around him*) Oh, Peter, Peter ... can't you see anything?

Peter I'm doing my best.

Pauline Your needs have changed in the last twenty-four hours.

Peter Have they?

Pauline Do you really have to have a running commentary from me on what you feel?

Peter Well, you seem to be the expert.

Pauline (*snuggling close*) On what?

Peter The battle of the sexes.

Pauline I'm not aware of any battle.

Peter You would be if Dad walked in now.

Pauline Tell me what your immediate need is, Peter.

Peter looks hard and long at her. Then he kisses her. She responds with determination. Peter manages to break from the clinch and crosses to the typewriter. He tries to regain his composure

Peter How did he think up the pen name Gerald B. Sharkey? What's the B stand for?

Pauline is slightly put out at having lost her quarry again

Pauline All you have to say now is that you enjoyed that.

Peter Well, it was ... nice.

Pauline (*sarcastically*) Gee whizz—was it really?

Peter (*confused*) But you r'e Dad's woman.

Pauline No. Martha is Dad's woman. Remember? I'm the wicked interloper.

Peter All the same ...

Pauline (*coaxingly*) Let's discuss the matter. (*She pats the settee beside her*)

Peter sits on the arm of the easy chair. Pauline continues to indicate the space on the settee. Peter goes to her and sits

Now, have you worked me out yet?

Peter (*gallantly*) I think ... you're a very wonderful person ...

Pauline Go on.

Peter And ... you're very beautiful ...

Pauline Yes?

Peter And I've never met anybody like you.

Pauline (*close to him*) And, bearing Harry in mind, do you accept that a man could give up everything to be with me?

Peter Yes, I could. Easily.

Pauline What about you?

Peter Yes ... I think I could.

Pauline Are you sure about that? (*She begins to massage Peter*)

Peter (*distracted by Pauline's wandering hands*) I think so.

Pauline Well, let's dispense with the running commentary. Let's have an action replay. (*She seizes Peter and kisses him with abandon*)

Peter offers no resistance and when the clinch breaks he looks at her smiling face

Peter (*rising abruptly*) This is ridiculous.

Pauline You do look faintly funny. (*She stretches out on the settee displaying a good deal of leg*)

Peter All right, you've had your bit of fun at my expense and I'm sure I've provided you with a good laugh ...

Pauline Poor Peter. The distressed virgin caught in the worst of all possible situations.

Peter I'm going.

Pauline Coward.

Peter (*going to the door* L) Yes, I am a coward.

Pauline Goodbye, Peter.

Peter Goodbye.

Peter exits L, *leaving the door open*

Pauline slowly rises and in a slow, deliberate way takes off her housecoat and puts it on the back of the easy chair. She then puts Peter's jacket on

Peter enters

Peter I left my ...

Peter sees Pauline wearing his jacket and looks at her imploringly. He moves towards her to recover his jacket but ...

Pauline turns and enters the bedroom, leaving the door open

(*Calling through the doorway*) Pauline, please take my jacket off. (*After a pause*) No, Pauline, just the jacket ... (*he hesitates at the doorway*)

Peter finally enters the bedroom and closes the door

The stage darkens for a moment to denote the passing of about two hours

When the lights return, Harry and Beaumont's voices are heard off, singing drunkenly

Harry and Beaumont enter L, *holding each other up. Harry is the worst affected*

Harry ⎫ (*together, singing*) Deutchland ... Deutchland ... uber alles ...
Beaumont ⎭ dum dee ... dum dee ... dum diddle dum ...

Harry collapses into an easy chair with a drunken laugh. Beaumont sits unsteadily on the arm of the settee

Harry Wilhelm, mein herr ...

Beaumont (*standing to attention, clicking his heels*) Ja, mein Kapitan? (*He rubs his ankle in pain*)

Harry Vat time isht?

Beaumont (*looking at his watch*) I do not know, mein Kapitan. Zis vatch only gives Munchengladbach time.

Harry That doesn't make sense.

Beaumont All right . . . you try saying Munchengladbach with a skinful. (*He flops back on the settee arm*)

Harry I've said enough tonight.

Beaumont But did you have to fight World War Two all over again with Gunter? I'm practically shell shocked.

Harry That's not shell shock. That's over indulgence of schnapps and sauerkraut.

Beaumont Good old Gunter.

Harry (*rising and going to the drinks cabinet*) I'll drink to that.

Beaumont No more for me.

Harry (*pouring a drink*) Aah . . . this is where we separate der kinder from der uberschtumfuhrers.

Beaumont I'm not in your league, Harry old mate.

Harry (*sitting on the settee L and raising his glass*) A toast.

Beaumont If you r'e going to drink to the downfall of women again—count me out. I love 'em.

Harry 'Course you do. That's why you're such a miserable bastard.

Beaumont (*with surprise*) Me? Miserable? I'm sweetness and light personi-fied.

Harry You're a bloody liar, Beaumont.

Beaumont Oh?

Harry Women have played havoc with your metab . . . metablies . . . metablers . . . your thing.

Beaumont What women?

Harry Last time I had a close look at Pauline she seemed to fit the description of female very well.

Beaumont (*protesting*) Pauline? You're barking up the wrong woman.

Harry You've been moping around ever since she left you. Old Harry sees all and hears all.

Beaumont And sees nicht.

Harry Admit I'm right, you scurrilous sample of snake venom.

Beaumont She'll always be true to you, Harry.

Harry I know.

Beaumont There's no question of her ever leaving you.

Harry (*rising and crossing to the bedroom door*) Well, let's put it to the little woman herself.

Beaumont crosses to Harry and gently pulls him to the easy chair

Beaumont Let the girl sleep. She's probably had a hard night.

Harry (*sitting in the easy chair*) Doing what?

Beaumont Well, I imagine she's had a good deal of pressure on her.

Harry Pressure?

Beaumont All this engagement business with your son and your wife's ghost being resurrected. It can't be easy for her to sleep with something like that weighing her down.

Harry (*scornfully*) Oh yes. I bet she's been wrestling with it all night.

Beaumont You're a selfish bastard, Ryder. You only see things in terms of your own involvement.

Harry Coming from you that's priceless. Save your platitudes. I've got my hands full at the moment *trying* to make a living.

Beaumont What about Pauline? Don't you think she's got her hands full just now?

Harry How do you mean?

Beaumont I mean ... putting up with a grouchy old boozer and actually *making* a living for both of you.

Harry My God, you really have got it bad for her, haven't you?

Beaumont It's time I went. You've had a busy day, Harry. I won't keep you from your loved one any longer.

Harry Sure you wouldn't like a drop of the hard stuff before you go?

Beaumont (*rising*) I'm sure. I'll off to my lonely bed. At least, you've got someone in there to give you a warm glow and rapturous welcome.

Harry And don't think I'm not thankful for that.

Beaumont (*crossing to the door* L) Auf Wiedersehen, mein Kapitan.

Harry Guten nacht, mein Herr.

Beaumont Unt gif der fraulein some schtick from me.

Beaumont exits

Harry hums "Deutchland uber Alles" as he pours a drink. He downs it and then quickly downs another one

Harry (*singing*) Ven der Führer says vee isht der master race, vee go Heil! Heil! Right in der Führer's face. (*He manages a goose step and collapses into the easy chair*) Mein Gott ... mein brain isht kaput. Harry, mein Herr, ich thinken isht time for der beddy bye byzen. Ja. Ish time for der cuddlesy uppen mit mein fraulein. (*He rises with difficulty and goes to the bedroom door*) Mein leibling ... here isht your dumbkopf Harry. (*He opens the bedroom door and peers in*) Mein leibling ... (*He closes the door quickly and looks stunned. He opens the door again and looks into the bedroom. Appalled, he closes the door and lurches to the settee*) Schwein-hunts ... Schweinhunts ... (*He mutters darkly to himself*)

CURTAIN

ACT II

Scene 1

The same. It is the same morning, a few hours later

Early morning sunlight shines through a gap in the curtains. As the Curtain *rises Harry is asleep on the settee. Pauline is sitting impassively on the arm of the easy chair as she looks at Harry*

Peter (*from the bedroom*) Pauline . . .
Pauline In here.

Peter enters. He is in the middle of dressing, putting on his tie

Peter How long have you been up? I . . . (*He sees Harry on the settee and goes for a closer look*)
Pauline (*flatly*) I've been up for some hours.
Peter Is he drunk or something?
Pauline Very drunk.
Peter I wonder if he . . . if he . . .
Pauline He saw us.
Peter How do you know?
Pauline I heard him come in. He was raving on in German. He'd obviously been to Gunter's place. He looked in the bedroom and I have the feeling he didn't like what he saw.
Peter (*hopefully*) But if he was drunk—he might not . . .
Pauline (*calmly*) He saw us.
Peter But . . . he might not have, well . . . caught on . . .
Pauline He didn't think we'd been playing Monopoly.
Peter (*miserably*) God . . . how did I let myself get into this?

Pauline rises and goes to the window then back to Peter

Pauline Because you're weak.
Peter What?
Pauline (*with a false smile*) Because of human weakness. (*She draws the curtains*)

Harry stirs

Peter What are we going to tell him?
Pauline Leave that to me.
Peter But you must have known what you were doing.
Pauline Me? Didn't you know?

Peter (*confused*) No, well ... yes ... but, Christ, you said ...

Pauline I think one short term need is for you to finish dressing.

Peter looks at Pauline and then Harry in hopeless desperation, then exits to the bedroom

Harry stirs again. Pauline goes to him and speaks quietly in his ear

Harry. Harry, wake up. Come on. Face the world and all its realities.

Harry's eyes blink open. He struggles to sit up and winces dramatically with pain as he holds his head

Harry Christ, somebody get that herd of buffalo out of here.

Pauline (*soothingly*) Poor, naughty Harry. What has he inflicted on himself this time?

Harry (*taking in his situation, seeing the blanket*) What's this ...? What ...? (*He stares at Pauline*) You ... you ...

Pauline (*softly*) I think you'd better take it easy, darling.

Harry (*growing angry*) Don't "darling" me. Where's Peter? (*He makes a move to rise*)

Pauline (*gently pushing him back*) You stay here. Muhammad will come to the mountain soon enough.

Harry What's going on, Pauline?

Pauline I should have thought that was obvious even to someone in your state. You know, I think drink will be the end of you someday.

Harry (*irritably*) Never mind my drinking habits. What about one or two of your habits?

Pauline (*with studied innocence*) Whatever do you mean, Harry?

Harry Stop pussyfooting around with me. It's only my weakened condition that stops me from giving you a boot where it will do most good, you ... whore.

Pauline (*serenely*) Such righteous indignation. More in keeping with an insecure little accountant than a sophisticated literary giant.

Harry But why, Pauline? Why?

Pauline You've just said why. I'm a whore.

Harry (*chastened*) I didn't mean it. But will you please tell me why?

Pauline (*simply*) I love him. And he loves me.

Harry (*forcefully*) Rubbish.

Pauline Why?

Harry It's just too unbelievable.

Pauline It's a common enough occurrence.

Harry (*bewildered*) But you only met him for the first time last week. And anyway, your type just doesn't fall in love with his type.

Pauline I don't see how you can reach that conclusion. We have a lot in common. (*She smiles*) You could say we have many needs in common.

Harry What are you trying to do to me? You know how much you mean to me.

Pauline Don't let your imagination run away with you.

Harry Pauline ...

Pauline (*calling out to Peter*) All right, Muhammad, you can come in now.
You don't have to listen to any more.

Peter enters sheepishly. He is fully dressed

Peter (*avoiding Harry's gaze*) Hallo, Dad.

Peter feels self-conscious as Harry and Pauline look steadily at him. He fiddles with the paper in the typewriter and any other available object

How are you feeling? You don't look too good ... I'm ... I'm sorry about
the way the party turned out. ... It ... er ... wasn't such a good idea, was
it? I ... think you might have been right ... about not going, I mean. (*He
glances at Pauline but her expression reveals nothing*) I made a mad dash to
come and see you. I ... I ... suppose I felt sorry for you. I wanted to
explain that I saw your side of things a little better than I did ... I mean
... well ... you behaved badly but there was no need for Uncle Simon to
say the things he did ... and Mum ... well, I can only apologize for her.
She had a headache, you see and ... anyway ... I just wanted to talk to
you. ...

Harry (*after a studied pause*) That was a pretty speech. Wasn't that a pretty
speech, Pauline?

Pauline (*in a deadpan voice*) Yes. Now I have a little speech to make.

Harry Oh good. I hope it's less excruciating than the one we've just had to
endure.

Pauline You're terribly shocked at finding Peter and me in bed together. It
may be a genuine shock or all a sham—I'm never sure with you. But
before you recover from it I would just like to beat you to the punch and
tell you not to blame Peter for what's happened. You needn't bother
blaming me, either. Surely you didn't think you'd get away with it forever.
You needn't look so puzzled. You're your own worst enemy, Harry.
You've ruined Peter's life, Martha's life and you've ruined mine. And by
doing that you've brought me and Peter together. If you can't see that
then you're not half as bright as you've always pretended to be.

Harry (*incredulously*) What's all this talk about ruining lives? You've been
happy with me ... haven't you?

Pauline How can I be happy with someone who's more like a baby than a
grown man? Always demanding flattery, crying out for attention. A man
who thinks that because he changes his name to Gerald B. Sharkey he's
thrown out the past and can forget his failings.

Harry I've never claimed to be perfect ...

Pauline You can't even make a living.

Harry (*quietly*) I see. So that's it.

There is a long pause

Well, then. What now? Do we all behave like rational people and discuss
the matter?

Pauline (*going to the L of Peter*) For once you are one step behind the event.
Peter and I have decided what's to be done.

Peter (*with surprise*) Have we?

Pauline Yes, we have.

Peter What did we decide?

Pauline You said you wanted to go away with me. To take me away from here.

Peter Did I? I don't . . .

Pauline You really do love me, don't you?

Peter (*on the spot*) Well, I . . .

Pauline Last night wasn't just a tumble in the hay with a wicked woman, was it?

Peter 'Course not.

Pauline And you really meant it when you said I should go with you and lead our lives together?

Peter Honestly, Pauline, I don't remember . . .

Pauline Why do you think I've got my suitcase packed?

Harry (*with alarm*) Pauline, you're not going now? Right now?

Pauline While you two snored your heads off I've been preparing for my new life.

Pauline goes into the bedroom

Peter looks helplessly at Harry

Pauline re-enters carrying two suitcases which she puts beside the easy chair

They're on the heavy side. You'd better carry them, Peter.

Peter, without thinking, picks up the suitcases

I've got nothing of yours, Harry. Anything of mine I've left behind you can keep in memory of the days when you had a serf working for you.

Harry (*rising, the implications having finally got through to him*) I can't believe this. It can't be happening. You've never shown a callous streak before.

Pauline (*doggedly*) There's an old saying about being cruel to be kind.

Pauline takes hold of Peter's hand and leads him to the front door

Harry (*pleading pathetically*) Pauline, please, let's talk about this. All right, so you've humiliated me . . . maybe you think I had that coming to me. I don't know. But for God's sake, Pauline . . . don't go—not this very minute. I may be all the things you said I am—but what can I be without you? I'll be nothing. I'm begging you, Pauline, stay. Let's talk it over. Peter, you're taking my life away from me. Surely I haven't done anything to deserve this. You'll be killing me. I love you, Pauline. You must still love me a little. Please Pauline, don't go. Stay. I need you, Pauline. I need you. (*He ends up in a crouching position, in tears*)

Pauline appears to be unmoved. Peter is visibly shaken

Pauline (*to Peter, flatly*) Now you know what the B stands for.

Pauline hustles Peter through the door, Peter giving a last look of concern as they exit

Harry remains on his knees looking forlornly at the floor

Black-out

SCENE 2

The same. About a week later. Morning

Harry enters L carrying bottles of drink. He places them by the kitchen sink, then crosses to the typewriter

Harry (*reading*) "Come in, Mr Steele, I've been expecting you." (*He thinks for a moment then puts the cover over the typewriter wearily*) Go to sleep, Larry. I've lost interest in you.

There is a knock at the door

Enter!

Allan Beaumont enters. He is quite chirpy

Beaumont Morning, you old reprobate. How's your day going?
Harry (*unenthusiastically*) Like a nuclear holocaust.
Beaumont Glad to hear it.
Harry And what brings you here? Checking on my progress with Larry Steele?
Beaumont No.
Harry That's just as well, because there hasn't been any progress.
Beaumont That doesn't really surprise me.
Harry And there won't be any more.
Beaumont What does that mean?
Harry It means Gerald B Sharkey has written his last line of trash. Larry Steele has had his last screw, Boris Prendergast has garrotted his last victim. I've dotted my last T and crossed my last I. No more will the world be assaulted by the meaningless outpourings of a misguided, untalented literary clown. All is finis, kaput, terminated.
Beaumont Just as well.
Harry Is that your only comment?
Beaumont What do you think I should say?
Harry You could try "Don't do it, Harry, the world needs you to go on."
Beaumont All right—don't do it, Harry, the world needs you to go on.
Harry Cobblers.
Beaumont (*after a pause*) What should I say now?
Harry Don't say anything. Have you got any booze at home?
Beaumont Yes. Why?
Harry Go around and get it.
Beaumont Then what?
Harry Bring it round here, you berk.

Beaumont I see. Gerald B. Sharkey is going out in a great big splash of alcohol.

Harry Right. He's going to be drowned in a sea of booze. And we might as well start now. (*He pours drinks into two glasses*)

Beaumont I can't say that I'm familiar with the burial service at sea. How do you perform the last rites?

Harry You say "Farewell, Gerald B. Sharkey—old friend, pseud and twit. May the herrings have mercy on your soul."

Beaumont (*taking a glass and singing*) There's a plaice for you—two conger eels and a plaice for you.

Harry I must say you're taking it all very calmly.

Beaumont I think you've made a wise decision.

Harry You're not worried about losing all that lovely loot?

Beaumont Well, let's face it, Harry ...

Harry I know—I've hardly lined any pockets. A few brows maybe, but definitely no pockets.

Beaumont You'll go back to Martha, of course.

Harry Why should I?

Beaumont Well, it seems the logical thing to do.

Harry What's logical about it?

Beaumont Well, you've got to think of your future, Harry. She wants you back and I, for one, think it's a damned good idea.

Harry Oh, you do, do you?

Beaumont Yes.

Harry So you think the cold and hungry escaped prisoner should give himself up, eh?

Beaumont What?

Harry Nothing.

Beaumont And, of course, you must think of Pauline.

Harry (*ironically*) Oh yes, I must think of Pauline.

Beaumont You don't have to worry on that score, old mate. I'll see that she'll be all right.

Harry I can rely on that, can I?

Beaumont Naturally. I dare say she'll be a bit cut up about it at first—but she's a realist.

Harry You're quite a realist yourself, Allan.

Beaumont I try to be.

Harry You've got the whole scenario already figured out, haven't you? Me slowly chugging out of Euston Station on a fast Inter-City while Pauline tearfully waves a last farewell with your consoling arm around her waist. Then it's back to your flat, drop 'em and into the sack. Then afterwards mumble something about good old Harry doing the right thing.

Beaumont Harry, I've never hidden my feelings for Pauline. I love her. Oh, I know she's your girl but ...

Harry Don't rave on and make a bloody fool of yourself. Pauline's gone.

Beaumont What do you mean—gone?

Harry She's run off with another fellow.

Beaumont You're having me on.

Harry Unfortunately I'm not.

Beaumont Who is he?

Harry A bloke by the name of Peter Ryder.

Beaumont (*stunned*) Not ... not Peter Ryder? Your son?

Harry The same. She waltzed out of here a week ago declaring her undying love for him.

Beaumont But I thought you told me he was a bit of a schmuck—especially with women.

Harry Well, he's got something you and I lack. What's more important he's got Pauline.

Beaumont I can't believe it.

Harry You'd better believe it, baby.

Beaumont What's happened to her judgement?

Harry It does make you wonder, doesn't it? Passing up two wonderful lovers like us for a callow mother's boy.

Beaumont You've got to try to get her back, Harry.

Harry How do you suggest I do that?

Beaumont Go to Batley or Bootle or wherever it is and drag her back.

Harry It's Burnley—and I have no intentions of dragging her back.

Beaumont I thought she was your whole life?

Harry She is, you bloody idiot—or was. But I haven't the right.

Beaumont That doesn't sound like you. What right had your son to ...

Harry He had every right—just as Martha has every right to try to get me back. The only one with no rights is me.

Beaumont What the hell are you talking about, Harry?

Harry I had no right to walk out on her.

Beaumont I never thought I'd see the day when I would hear you spouting such bloody drivel.

Harry It makes a change from writing it.

Beaumont If you feel that way why aren't you back in Martha's caring arms right now?

Harry Don't think I haven't given that question some thought.

Beaumont (*shaking his head*) The rotten little tramp ...

Harry How about going for that drink?

Beaumont (*oblivious*) The two-faced, flint-hearted little tramp ...

Harry Allan.

Beaumont What?

Harry The bottles of comfort. Go and get them.

Beaumont (*going to the door* L) Right. But we've got to sort something out. We can't let her get away with it. Agreed?

Harry (*wearily*) Just do your errand.

Beaumont We'll discuss it when I get back. (*To himself. With great feeling*) The degenerate, heartless little tramp ...

Beaumont exits

Harry wanders aimlessly around the room. He pours a drink, takes a book from the shelf and sits on the arm of the settee. He idly flips through the book, slams it shut and returns it to the shelf. He opens the window and braces himself against the expected noise. But there is no sound of Alistair's saxophone. He leaves the window open and moves towards the bedroom

There is a knock on the door. Harry crosses and opens it

Peter stands in the doorway. He looks sheepish

Harry If it isn't young Lochinvar come out of the North.
Peter Hallo Dad. Can I come in?
Harry What have you come for this time? The silverware?
Peter Look, Dad . . .
Harry (*crossing* R) Come in—and bring the light of your life with you.

Peter enters

Peter (*closing the door*) If you mean Pauline—she isn't with me.
Harry You mean you're not returning the soiled goods?
Peter No, Dad.
Harry She's not with you?
Peter No.
Harry Where the hell is she!
Peter I don't know.
Harry What d'you mean—you don't know?
Peter I mean—I don't know.
Harry For God's sake, you can't mislay something of Pauline's proportions—even you.
Peter Do you think I could have a drink of something?
Harry Help yourself to the cyanide.
Peter Thanks. (*He pours a drink*)
Harry (*feigning indifference*) Anyway, if you think the whereabouts or activities of that particular female concern me you're mistaken, son.
Peter Really?
Peter Yes. I've completely banished her from my mind.
Peter Is that true?
Harry Would I lie to you?
Peter I don't know.
Harry She's your responsibility now. I'm well rid of her.
Peter Dad . . . I've come to tell you . . .
Harry I don't want to discuss her, Peter.
Peter (*slightly rattled*) On my first visit you didn't want to discuss Mum. Now on this visit you don't want to discuss Pauline.
Harry It was your second visit I could have done without.
Peter Aren't you even a little bit interested?
Harry Look Peter, I don't know what you expected to find here. You probably thought I'd have my head in the gas oven or that I'd have committed hara-kiri. Well, sorry to disappoint you.
Peter I don't know what I expected.
Harry So you've satisfied yourself that I'm alive and well. Now you can get back to Pauline and your idyllic love life.
Peter I've told you I don't know where she is.

Harry So what do you want from me? A radar scanner? A Geiger counter? A pack of bloodhounds?

Peter You really like to make things awkward for me, don't you?

Harry Your presence here is no more welcome than on the two previous occasions.

Peter If that means . . .

Harry It means "go".

Peter Look, Dad, I know your opinion of me isn't very high . . .

Harry Ten out of ten for observation.

Peter And I probably deserve it . . .

Harry Eleven out of ten for judgement.

Peter But it took a lot of guts for me to come and see you today.

Harry None out of ten for common sense.

Peter (*getting overheated*) You can be as sarcastic as you like—I've got something to tell you and I'm bloody well going to tell you.

Harry Don't you raise your voice to me, son.

Peter And don't you threaten me.

Harry Don't think I can't still give you a paternal good hiding.

Peter I'm not a little boy any more.

Harry You're still young enough.

Peter But old enough to take your girl friend away from you.

Harry (*subsiding*) That remark just earned you full marks for truthfulness. All right, tell me all about it.

Peter Well, we'd gone about twenty miles out of London when Pauline said "Let's have some breakfast." So we stopped at a small café. We'd just finished our bacon and eggs when she said she wanted something out of the car. When she didn't show up after about quarter of an hour I went to look for her. She'd disappeared.

Harry Did you find her?

Peter Yes. Eventually.

Harry Where?

Peter On the local railway station with her suitcase. She was waiting for a London train.

Harry Go on.

Peter Well, naturally I asked her for an explanation.

Harry Naturally.

Peter And she told me it was all for the well-being and happiness of the one man she loved.

Harry (*puzzled*) Meaning you?

Peter No. Meaning you.

Harry Me?

Peter I was as surprised as you. I reminded her of the pitiful state you were in when we left you . . .

Harry (*aggrieved*) I wasn't pitiful . . .

Peter You were pathetic. Anyway, I said, "What about me?" And do you know what she said?

Harry I couldn't hazard a guess.

Peter She said she despised me as much as she loved you.

Harry Are you sure that's what she said?

Peter Positive. She said I nauseated her.

Harry That was a dramatic change of heart in one hour.

Peter That's what I said. Anyway, she seems to think she's helping you somehow.

Harry (*pondering this*) Helping me?

Peter I wouldn't worry too much about it, Dad. As you said—you're well rid of her.

Harry Where did she say she would go?

Peter She just said she'd probably go back to her husband.

Harry And she said that everything she'd done was for my happiness?

Peter Yes. She's got a twisted mind if you ask me.

Harry It's all very puzzling ...

Peter She's played us both for fools.

Harry (*to himself*) What motive could she possibly have had?

Peter Forget her, Dad. She's not worth bothering about. Just forget her.

Harry (*incredulous*) Forget her?

Peter Yes. For your own peace of mind.

Harry Peace of mind? Peace of mind? Let me show you something.

Harry goes into the bedroom and returns with a small overnight bag and moves R *of the settee*

How much peace of mind do you think I can have when she's left this sort of thing here? (*He pulls a negligé from the bag and throws it over Peter's head. He then drapes a pair of tights around Peter's shoulders*) And how conducive to my peace of mind do you suppose this is? (*He holds aloft a bra*)

Peter (*taking the garments off himself*) Can't you give them to somebody?

Harry All my transvestite friends have deserted me, I'm afraid. (*He places the bra on the typewriter chair*)

Peter (*steeling himself*) Dad ...

Harry (*putting the negligé and tights back in the bag*) What?

Peter There's ... there's something else I have to tell you.

Harry Oh?

Harry takes the bag into the bedroom

Peter Yes. Mum and Cheryl are in my car outside.

Harry enters, minus the bag, his face aghast

(*Quickly*) You see, Mum suggested we all have a week away in Bournemouth, so we packed our bags and off we went.

Harry And your mother just happened to say "Let's pop in on your father while we're down here."

Peter Yes ... I mean ... I did, really.

Harry Liar. It was Martha's idea.

Peter Anyway, I don't see what harm it would do just to see her.

Harry She had her chance to see me at the party.

Peter And you can meet Cheryl again.

Harry I wasn't very impressed with her on our one and only encounter.
Peter Come on, Dad, that's not fair. You only saw her for a few minutes.
Harry God, Peter, why don't you give up?
Peter Give up what?
Harry Trying to get me back to the fold.
Peter Is it all right if I bring them up?
Harry (*with a deep sigh*) Why do I keep getting this feeling of being backed into a corner?
Peter Well, is it all right?
Harry (*with resignation*) I suppose so.
Peter (*going to the door* L) Oh by the way, Dad ... I didn't tell them about last week. They don't know anything about me and Pauline.
Harry That's a very guilty secret to have to keep.
Peter You won't say anything, will you?
Harry Your little escapade won't be revealed by me.
Peter (*relieved*) Thanks.

Peter exits

Harry frantically tries to hide any appearance of poverty. He throws bottles into a box, puts them in the kitchen area and draws the curtain concealing the kitchen. He spruces himself up in front of the mirror

There is a knock at the door

Harry answers it

Martha, Cheryl and Peter enter in varying degrees of embarrassment and self-consciousness

Harry Hallo, Martha.
Martha Hallo, Harry.
Harry Hallo, Cheryl.
Cheryl (*in a deadpan voice*) Hallo.
Harry (*trying to joke*) Welcome to Ryder's Hall of Residence. Sit down everybody.

Martha and Cheryl sit on the settee. Peter sits on the easy chair. Harry goes to sit on the typewriter chair, sees the bra on it and hurriedly puts it behind the typewriter. He sits on the chair facing the others. There is an awkward silence

Peter (*to Martha*) I told Dad we're going to Bournemouth for a week.
Harry Yes ... that should be very nice.
Martha Yes.
Peter Yes ... it's very nice ... in Bournemouth.
Harry Yes ... you should have a nice time.
Martha Yes.
Peter It makes a change.
Harry Yes ... it should be nice.
Peter Have you ever been to Bournemouth?
Harry No ... no, I've never been there ... but I've heard it's very nice.
Peter Yes.

Martha Yes.

Cheryl (*to Harry*) Do you have such a thing as a loo?

Harry Pardon?

Cheryl I'm busting. (*She points at Peter*) Dreamboat here couldn't find a public toilet anywhere.

Harry (*rising and opening the door on the* L) It's out through here to the left.

Cheryl (*rising and crossing to the door*) I've been on the verge of wetting myself for the last half hour. (*She points at Peter*) He wouldn't care.

Cheryl exits

Martha A very nice girl, Cheryl.

Harry Oh yes ... a real charmer.

Martha Her father's very high up at Fowler's Engineering.

Harry Is he really?

Martha Yes.

Peter (*to Harry*) You probably remember him—Jimmy Bradshaw.

Harry I don't know him.

Peter You must do. Little fellow with a slight limp and a Cortina.

Harry I don't know him.

Peter (*persistently*) He's in the office. Little bloke—plays a lot of bowls.

Harry And you talk a lot of it. Now shut up. I don't know him.

Martha (*to Harry*) You've changed.

Harry Have I?

Martha Yes. You've aged.

Harry That's a process we all go through.

Martha But you've aged a lot.

Harry Five years to be precise.

Martha Do you live here alone?

Harry Yes.

Martha Nobody lives here with you?

Harry No.

Martha Are you sure?

Harry (*slightly rattled*) What a damned silly question. 'Course I'm sure.

Peter (*intervening*) How's the latest novel going, Dad?

Harry It's going very well.

Peter Good.

Harry Yes. I've got high hopes for it.

Martha You're still writing then?

Harry Of course I am. That's my livelihood.

Martha Oh ... I thought ...

Harry You thought what?

Martha Nothing.

Harry (*after a pause*) Good journey?

Martha } (*together*) { Terrible.
Peter } { Very good.

Harry (*after a pause*) What was the weather like up north?

Martha } (*together*) { Awful.
Peter } { Not bad.

Martha (*after a pause*) We won't be staying long.

Harry No, 'course not. You'll be pretty keen to get on your way ... I imagine.

Martha Yes.

Peter We just popped in.

Harry Yes ... I appreciate it.

Cheryl enters. She resumes her position on the settee

Cheryl (*to Harry*) This place is a bit of a dump, isn't it?

Harry You think so?

Cheryl Compared to the lovely home you had in Burnley it's a hovel.

Peter I don't think ...

Cheryl (*to Harry*) Do you share the loo with the other tenants?

Harry On this floor, yes.

Cheryl Well, I think you should club together for a new light bulb in there. The one in there now has gone.

Harry How can it be in there now if it's gone?

Cheryl It's blown—not working. I couldn't see my hand in front of my face.

Harry I wouldn't have thought it was particularly important to see your hand in there. Not in front of your face, anyway.

Peter (*to Cheryl, with concern*) Did you manage all right, pet?

Cheryl After getting my knickers in a lot of twists I finally managed.

Harry (*to Peter*) Yes, son, a real charmer.

Peter (*rising*) Well, do you think we ought to go?

Martha Well ...

Cheryl Why?

Peter Well, Dad probably wants to get some writing done and ...

Cheryl Oh shut up and sit down.

Harry (*striving to keep calm*) If you don't mind, young lady, in this flat I'll give the orders.

Cheryl Then tell him to shut up and sit down.

Harry (*to Peter*) Do you want to go?

Peter Well, I just thought it might be an idea to ...

Harry Why don't you bloody well go?

Peter (*to Martha*) Mum?

Martha What, dear?

Peter Do you want to go?

Martha Well, I suppose ...

Harry You may as well know you're not welcome here.

Cheryl That's a nice thing to say. After we've come all this way.

Martha (*to Harry*) You've made it perfectly obvious we aren't welcome, Harry.

Harry Then do the sensible thing and leave me alone.

Cheryl You shouldn't talk to her like that. Mrs Ryder thinks the world of you, you know. You're a very lucky man and you don't realize it.

Harry Oh for God's sake ...

Cheryl It's true. She has a photo of you on the china cabinet and one on her dressing-table.

Harry And one tattooed on her chest?

Martha You've always got great pleasure out of being cruel to me, haven't you?

Cheryl I don't know why you bother about him, Mrs Ryder. Let him rot in this pigsty.

Harry Some little girls don't know when to keep their mouths shut.

Cheryl And some old men don't know when they're well off.

Harry Peter. You'd better call her off.

Peter Come on Cheryl ... please. You promised you wouldn't cause a scene.

Cheryl I can't help it. It makes my blood boil to think how he's treated your mother. And to think she wants him back.

Martha Please, Cheryl, I can fight my own battles.

Harry Oh, if it's a battle you want ...

There is a knock at the door. Harry answers it

Beaumont enters carrying several bottles. He places them in the kitchen area

Beaumont Ready to sink the *Titanic*?

Harry Allan, this is Martha, my wife. Allan Beaumont.

Beaumont (*with extreme courtesy*) Very pleased to meet you.

Harry And this is Cheryl, my son's fiancée.

Beaumont A great pleasure.

Harry And this is my son, Peter.

Beaumont's pleasant attitude suddenly changes to fury. He grabs Peter by the jacket lapels and shakes him furiously

Beaumont (*to Peter*) Where is she? Where is she? You swine. What have you done with her?

Peter (*uncomprehending*) Where's who?

Beaumont Don't play innocent with me. You know who. Pauline. Where's Pauline?

Harry drags Beaumont away from Peter and propels him to the door L

Harry Allan, old mate, you haven't brought a corkscrew. Go and get one.

Beaumont Corkscrew?

Harry Yes, corkscrew. Off you go.

Harry pushes Beaumont out and closes the door

Cheryl What was all that about? Who's Pauline?

Peter (*desperately*) Er ... she's, well ...

Harry (*with inspiration*) She's a whippet.

Martha A whippet?

Harry Yes. She's Allan's favourite black whippet!

Cheryl Has he lost her?

Harry Er ... in a way yes.

Cheryl But why should Peter know where she is?

Peter Well, you see ... it's like this ...

Harry When Peter was up here last week Allan let him take Pauline for a romp in the park, didn't he, Peter?

Peter That's right.

Cheryl And you lost her?

Peter I'm afraid so.

Harry Well, Pauline always was a bit frisky and she was on heat, wasn't she?

Peter Er ... yes, she was.

Harry So Peter couldn't handle her and she probably ran off with some big, macho Alsatian.

Peter I couldn't do much about it, I'm afraid.

Harry But I can't blame Allan for being upset. She was a lovely little bitch.

There is a loud knocking on the door. Harry answers it

Beaumont enters. He is very irate

Beaumont What are you talking about—corkscrew? You've got about half a dozen bloody corkscrews.

Harry You know—I think you're right.

Beaumont (*to Peter*) All right, come on. No evasions. Where's Pauline?

Peter I don't know.

Beaumont You don't know?

Harry That's right. He doesn't know.

Beaumont He's lying. He must know.

Cheryl Why should he lie? She got lost.

Beaumont Lost?

Cheryl Yes.

Beaumont Where?

Cheryl In the park.

Harry Look Allan, why don't you go home and we can discuss this another time?

Beaumont I want to discuss it now with him.

Peter Why? What was she to you?

Beaumont I love her.

Harry Oh come on, Allan. Let's not get carried away.

Beaumont I don't see why you are so calm. She did share your bed as well as mine.

Martha Did she?

Beaumont Yes. And now pipsqueak here steals her away ...

Martha Peter hasn't stolen anything.

Cheryl He certainly didn't bring her to Burnley with him.

Beaumont So you expect me to believe that she got lost in the park?

Cheryl Why not? It happens all the time. Especially when they're on heat.

Beaumont You'd better watch it.

Harry Calm down, Allan, old mate.

Martha Yes. It seems to me you're making a lot of fuss about nothing.

Beaumont Nothing? I tell you I love her.

Martha I'm sure you did. But Peter will replace her.

Beaumont Replace her? Who with? (*He indicates Cheryl*) Minnie Mouse here?

Cheryl This Pauline must have been worth a lot. Did she win a lot of money?

Beaumont I don't know what your game is but you'd better lay off insulting Pauline.

Cheryl Peter, for God's sake, give him some money for her and let's hear the end of it.

Beaumont You think you can buy me off? (*He sees Pauline's bra. He crosses and holds it up*) Ha—ha. She's here, isn't she? This is Pauline's. I'd know it anywhere. (*He throws down the bra*) Where is she? In the bedroom?

Beaumont storms into the bedroom

Harry (*picking up the bra*) It's . . . er . . . they're . . . they're blinkers.

Martha Blinkers?

Harry Yes. Whippets wear blinkers sometimes. (*To Peter*) Don't they?

Peter (*wearily*) I suppose so.

Cheryl What are whippet's blinkers doing here?

Beaumont enters

Beaumont She's not in there. Come on Harry. You know what's going on.

Harry I only know you're making a bloody fool of yourself.

Cheryl (*to Harry*) Why should you have Pauline's blinkers?

Harry I looked after her for a while.

Beaumont (*snorting*) In a fashion.

Martha Have you advertised in the paper for her?

Beaumont Very funny.

Cheryl That's a very good idea.

Beaumont You're all off your heads.

Cheryl We're only trying to be helpful.

Beaumont Your beloved fiancé here is the only one who can help.

Cheryl It wasn't Peter's fault. You should have trained her better.

Beaumont Oh, it's my fault, is it?

Cheryl Peter couldn't help it if she fancied a big Alsatian.

Beaumont What the hell are you talking about?

Cheryl I'm talking about your stupid black bitch.

Beaumont lunges angrily at Cheryl. Harry and Peter drag him off with difficulty

Harry Come on now, Allan lad. I think you'd better go home and cool off.

Martha (*with disgust*) I should think so.

Beaumont (*giving up the struggle and calming down*) All right. Let go. I'm going. I wouldn't stay with this family of vipers for another minute.

Harry That's the idea, Allan.

Beaumont All I can say to you, Harry, is that it's a good thing you've had the sense to give up writing. You were never any good. Get back where you belong—among soul-less cyphers like these three specimens of human dross. (*Mustering great dignity*) I bid you all ... good day.

Beaumont exits

Cheryl Well, I've seen some performances in my time ...
Harry I'm afraid Allan is a little overwrought just now.
Cheryl He's definitely over something.
Harry And now I'd appreciate it if you followed his example and left.
Martha If you're not writing novels now, what are you doing?
Harry Who says I'm not writing?
Martha He did.
Harry Well, he's wrong.
Martha The cover's on the typewriter.
Harry (*removing the typwriter cover*) So? The lid's on the saucepan but that doesn't mean I've stopped eating.

Peter crosses to the typewriter and reads

Peter "Come in, Mr Steele, I've been expecting you." That's as far as you'd got the last time I was here.
Harry (*meaningfully*) And how far did *you* get the last time you were here?
Peter Why don't you admit it's all over, Dad?
Harry The writing? All right, it's all over.
Cheryl So what are you going to do now? Play with your Meccano set?
Peter (*softly*) Come back home with us, Dad. Please.
Harry My answer to that is the same as before, Peter. Nothing's changed.
Peter But it has. A lot has changed.
Harry You mean Pauline!
Peter Er ... yes.
Cheryl Oh not that bloody whippet again.
Harry Do I have to ask you again to leave me alone? Go. Now.
Peter Come on, Mum. Let's go.
Cheryl (*rising*) Yes, come on Mrs Ryder. You're not doing any good here. He's not worth bothering about.
Peter (*exploding*) Oh for Christ's sake, Cheryl, why don't you shut your mouth?
Cheryl I believe in speaking my mind.
Peter It's a pity you don't employ your brains at the same time.
Cheryl (*with shock*) Peter!
Peter I'm sick to death of listening to you go raving on about something you know absolutely nothing about.
Cheryl Oh is that so?
Peter Yes—that is so. Why don't you have a go at fixing up your own parent's marriage before you start on mine?
Cheryl My mum and dad are very happy, thank you.
Peter Like hell they are.
Cheryl My dad hasn't left Mum in the lurch after taking the best years of her life from her.

Peter That's because your father couldn't find his way to the bathroom without a detailed road map.

Cheryl At least he doesn't lose whippets in the park.

Peter I didn't lose a whippet.

Cheryl What was it then? A Bengal tiger?

Peter Pauline is a woman. A very beautiful, intelligent woman.

Harry Righto, you two. Drop it.

Peter (*to Cheryl*) I spent a night with her. And it was the greatest night of my life.

Cheryl Where?

Peter (*pointing to the bedroom*) In there.

Cheryl (*to Harry*) You disgusting old man. You set your son up with a woman in your own bedroom.

Peter Dad didn't know.

Cheryl But you're engaged to me.

Peter So what?

Cheryl So where is this prostitute now?

Peter She's a finer person than you could ever be.

Cheryl Well, you go after her then if she's so wonderful.

Peter I only wish I could.

Cheryl Don't think I'm going to stop you. (*She puts her engagement ring on the coffee table*) You can have that back and go on your merry way.

Peter Thanks. I couldn't have married a girl my father didn't approve of anyway.

Cheryl (*sneering*) Some father. He hasn't given you a thought in five years.

Peter (*looking at Harry*) He still knows me better than I know myself.

Cheryl (*to Harry*) Are you satisfied now?

Harry I shouldn't be—but I am.

Cheryl You should be proud of yourself.

Harry Proud?

Cheryl You've turned him against me. You've made him just like you.

Peter Why don't you shut up.

Cheryl Right. When you come crawling back I'll decide whether to forgive you or not.

Peter That's mighty big of you.

Cheryl You're acting very smart now but we'll see.

Peter All right, we'll see.

Cheryl I've had enough of this place. I'll wait in the car for you, Mrs Ryder.

Martha We won't be very long, Cheryl.

Cheryl (*to Peter*) You can give me a full explanation of this Pauline affair on the drive south.

Cheryl exits

Martha (*to Peter*) You've upset her now.

Peter What about me?

Martha I think you behaved very badly. I've never known you to act that way . . . ever.

Peter If you think I'm apologizing . . .

Martha I think you should.

Harry The lad's got nothing to be sorry about.

Martha That's a matter for his conscience to decide.

Peter Mum, let me tell you about Pauline ...

Martha You don't have to tell me. I know.

Harry How could you know?

Martha (*taking a letter from her handbag*) I've got a letter here. I got it about two months ago. Shall I read it out?

Harry (*puzzled*) If you must.

Martha (*reading*) "Dear Mrs Ryder, We have never met but we have both shared the affection of the same man—your husband, Harry. It has taken a great deal of soul searching and deliberation before I could bring myself to the difficult task of writing to you at this time. I love Harry greatly, but that does not blind me to the fact that he is becoming a mere shadow of what he once was. I have deluded myself long enough into thinking that his need for me was all he needed for his happiness. And make no mistake about this—Harry's happiness is of the greatest, paramount importance to me. But I now feel I must be practical. His writing talents are not great enough to sustain him through life—but he perseveres. I feel that as long as he has me he will continue to persevere—the inevitable result being misery and frustration for him. I cannot bring myself to simply leave him—not without knowing that his future held something to make up for his loss. So I have come to the conclusion—rightly or wrongly—that the only way for him to have any kind of future is with you—and his son who I know really means a good deal to him. He has sworn that he would never go back to you. But if you could manage, in some way, to convince him that he is loved and wanted and, above all, *needed* then the path may be smoothed for him to recapture something he once had. I am sure that you and Peter can provide him with a greater joy and contentment in the remainder of his life than I could ever hope to do. But Harry must be shown that this is true. I hope that your love for him is strong enough and your need to have him back real enough to show him that losing me and his literary goals are no great hardship. As for myself—I love him very much. But I am prepared to alienate him if I could be sure it would mean fulfilment for him. I hope that fulfilment lies with you—and the son he loves. Yours Pauline."

Harry (*stunned*) And so the engagement party plot was hatched.

Martha They were getting engaged anyway. It seemed like a good opportunity.

Peter Dad—I swear I knew nothing about this.

Martha That's true. Peter just carried out my orders. I didn't tell him about Pauline or this letter.

Peter But it would have been the decent thing to tell me about it. Do you think I'm still a child?

Martha In most things you are.

Harry (*still stunned*) And that's how you suddenly knew where I lived?

Martha She included this address—yes.

Harry Well, isn't life full of surprises?

Martha (*taking another letter from her bag*) I got this letter a few days ago. Shall I read it?
Peter Does it tell you about ... about her and me?
Martha Yes.
Peter Don't bother.
Harry So when the engagement party plot failed she had to resort to stronger methods. (*He looks at Peter*)
Martha The point now is—are you coming home, Harry?
Harry I'll have to think about it.
Martha You've had years to think about it. You're not in much of a position to start bargaining now.
Peter Mum, please ...
Martha Well, it's true. What is there to think about? There's nothing here for him.
Peter I know ... but, well he's had a bit of a shock.
Martha I had a bit of a shock when he walked out on me.
Peter I know, but ...
Martha You expect charity and understanding from me now just because the big adventure he set out on didn't quite work out. I always knew that, given time, he'd fall flat on his face and I'd have the job of patching him up again. Well, now he needs me and he knows it. Cheryl's not the only one who thinks I shouldn't bother with him. Your Uncle Simon thinks I'm mad. I probably am—but there you are—I'm too soft. (*To Harry*) I'll give you five minutes to make up your mind. I'll wait in the car.

Martha exits

Harry (*still stunned*) At the party she wouldn't come near me. Now she's come at me like a Kamikaze pilot.
Peter What are you going to do?
Harry I don't seem to have a lot of choice, do I?
Peter I suppose not.
Harry Aren't I lucky to have so many people committed to my happiness and welfare?
Peter I'm sorry, Dad.
Harry What about?
Peter I don't know.
Harry Yes ... well ...
Peter I'll wait outside with Mum.
Harry Right.

Peter exits L

Harry replaces the cover on the typewriter then puts the bottles and glasses in the kitchen area

Harry exits into the bedroom

Suddenly the sound of a saxophone comes through the window playing a recognizable tune

Harry enters carrying a suitcase. He puts the suitcase on the settee and opens it. It is empty. He goes to the window

Harry (*shouting*) That's my boy Alistair. Keep at it. You'll get there yet.

Harry exits into the bedroom

Peter enters L. *He carries his suitcase*

Harry enters from the bedroom carrying his socks and underwear. He sees Peter and stops suddenly

Peter (*putting his suitcase down*) How much is the rent on this place anyway?

Harry beams as he goes to Peter and takes his suitcase. He throws the suitcase into the bedroom and greets Peter in the middle of the room. They embrace

Harry I hope you've got enough to cover the two month's that's owing.

CURTAIN

FURNITURE AND PROPERTY LIST

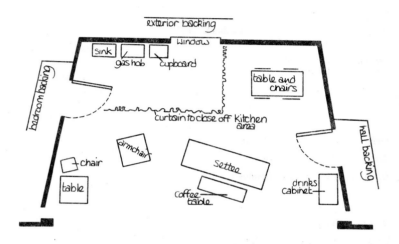

ACT I

SCENE 1

On stage: Large settee. *Under it:* handbag
Drinks cabinet: *In it:* various bottles and glasses
Table
Chairs
Pot plant. *In it:* bottle of vermouth
Small table. *On it:* typewriter with paper in the roller. *Under it:* **Harry**'s
   shoes
Coffee table
Easy chair
Bookshelf. *On it:* books, **Pauline**'s purse
Kitchen area. *In it:* sink, cupboard, kettle, gas hob, mugs, cutlery, coffee
Curtain to block off the kitchen area

Off stage: Matches, hairbrush, groceries **(Pauline)**
Jacket, carrier bag **(Harry)**
Groceries, shopping list **(Harry)**

Personal: **Peter:** invitation card in pocket

SCENE 2

Strike: Dirty glasses and mugs, typewriter, table and chair

Set: Small table. *On it:* various engagement presents including a coffee pot

Off stage: Glass of punch **(Peter)**

SCENE 3

Set: As for Scene I

Off stage: Housecoat, slippers **(Pauline)**
                  Matches **(Pauline)**

Personal: **Pauline:** watch
                  Bill: watch

ACT II

SCENE 1

Strike: Dirty glasses and mugs

Set: Blanket over **Harry**

Off stage: Two suitcases **(Pauline)**

SCENE 2

Strike: Blanket

Off stage: Bottles of drink **(Harry)**
                  Small overnight bag. *In it:* négligée, tights, bra **(Harry)**
                  Bottles of drink **(Bill)**
                  Suitcases **(Harry)**
                  Suitcase **(Peter)**
                  Socks and underwear **(Harry)**

Personal: **Cheryl:** engagement ring
                  Martha: handbag. *In it:* 2 letters

LIGHTING PLOT

Property fittings required: nil

2 Interiors: A furnished flat; an ante-room

ACT I
To open: Full general lighting

Cue 1   **Pauline** resumes putting the groceries away   (Page 18)
Black-out

Cue 2   As Scene 2 opens   (Page 18)
Lights up only on stage R

Cue 3   **Martha** and **Cheryl** exit with the table   (Page 24)
Black-out

Cue 4   As Scene 3 opens   (Page 24)
Dim lighting only

Cue 5   **Pauline** switches on the light   (Page 24)
Lights up

Cue 6   **Peter** enters the bedroom and closes the door   (Page 31)
Black-out for a moment only to denote the passing of time, then full Lights

ACT II

Cue 7   As Scene 1 opens   (Page 34)
Dim lighting with a light throwing sunlight through a gap in the curtains at the window

Cue 8   **Pauline** draws the curtains   (Page 34)
Lights up

Cue 9   **Harry** remains on his knees looking forlornly at the floor   (Page 38)
Black-out

Cue 10   As Scene 2 opens   (Page 38)
Lights up on **Harry**

EFFECTS PLOT

ACT I

Cue 1   **Harry** opens the window   (Page 1)
               Wailing of a saxophone wobbling up and down the scales

Cue 2   **Harry** closes the window   (Page 1)
               Saxophone stops

Cue 3   **Harry** opens the window   (Page 14)
               Wailing of a saxophone wobbling up and down the scales

Cue 4   **Harry** closes window   (Page 14)
               Saxophone stops

Cue 5   As Scene 2 opens and throughout this scene   (Page 18)
               Faint sound of a band playing

ACT II

Cue 6   **Harry** exits into the bedroom   (Page 33)
               Sound of a saxophone playing a recognizable tune

MADE AND PRINTED IN GREAT BRITAIN BY
LATIMER TREND & COMPANY LTD, PLYMOUTH
MADE IN ENGLAND